P
MAKING

"A week at. ⌐ ⌐ ⌐ ⌐ ⌐ ⌐ following Simone's system, I had an offer to write a book for a major publisher. The advance was equal to my total earnings for the previous year!"

April Elliott Kent
author, *Essential Guide to Practical Astrology*

"Combining feng shui principles with new moon magic, Simone offers a fine new spin on the tired old question, 'What shall we do with this new moon?' The benefits of her new moon practice are thoroughly researched and inspiring. If you'd like to shift the energy in your home and life, buy this book!"

Dana Gerhardt, columnist for
The Mountain Astrologer, Astrodienst

"Simone's unique combination of western astrological principles with the contemporary feng shui bagua is absolutely brilliant, and opens up a new level of practical applications for any home. I am excited about applying the new moon rituals to my home and life. In fact, I'll be cleaning up my desk in my Knowledge gua at the next new moon, which is my birthday—the perfect time to create an empowerment/intention ritual for the coming year."

Stephanie Roberts, author, *Fast Feng Shui* series

"It's puzzling to me that something this innocuous could be so powerful, but it proves itself month in and month out. I think it's directly tied to intention - what we intend and believe will happen, happens."

Sue Lemontre, Astro Feng Shui study participant

ABOUT THE AUTHOR

Simone Butler is an intuitive yet practical astrologer with more than 25 years of experience in helping people engage with the mystery of their lives. In addition to her consulting practice with clients worldwide, Simone has taught a variety of astrology classes, most recently at Vintage Religion in San Diego and the Golden Door in Escondido. Simone produced the daily forecasts for the *Starscroll* for many years. She now writes New and Full Moon forecasts for *www.Tarot.com.*

Astro Feng Shui, the system Simone developed in 2008, combines the ancient art of astrology with feng shui, as a user-friendly system for effecting change. Simone is certified by the Western School of Feng Shui. Her article on Astro Feng Shui was the Aug./Sept. 2009 cover story of *The Mountain Astrologer.*

Simone began her career as fashion editor for the *California Apparel News* in Los Angeles. Since then she has since written many articles, including celebrity interviews, for publications including *Outside Magazine, L.A. Times* and *San Diego Union-Tribune.* She served as arts editor for *THE TAB* in Sedona, and arts writer for *KPBS On Air Magazine* in San Diego. Simone's story, *Finding the Goddess in Zeus's Cave,* was published in **Greece: A Love Story** in 2007.

Simone currently lives in San Diego, California. She enjoys doing art and ritual, practicing yoga and salsa dancing. She awaits the love of her life to help her create an earthen home and sustainable community.

Contact Simone at: *www.astroalchemy.com* or *www.astrofengshui.net.*

Astro Feng Shui:
MAKING MAGIC IN YOUR HOME & LIFE

Copyright 2011 by Simone Butler.
All rights reserved.
No part of this book may be reproduced or used in any form,
including on the Internet, without written permission from the publisher, except in the case of brief quotations in articles or reviews.

Copyright 2011, in the United States of America

Portions of this book have been adapted from Simone Butler's Astro
Feng Shui report, and from her feature article in the Aug/Sept. 2009
issue of *The Mountain Astrologer*.

Cover design by Tish McAllise Sjoberg
Book layout by Florence Jones
Photo of Simone Butler by Amalya Peck
Published by Simone Butler, *www.astrofengshui.net*

CONTENTS

∝∾

*This book is dedicated to my mother,
Kay Hewes Butler (1920-2005) who
would have been so proud to welcome her
daughter's first book.*

*With gratitude to my editor, Shinan
Barclay, who tightens and tones my
sentences until they sing! Heartfelt thanks to
April Elliott Kent, Jannine Oberg, Florence
Jones and Tish McAllise Sjoberg, for their
help with graphics, ideas and inspiration.
And, great appreciation to my friends and
clients who performed Astro Feng Shui rituals in their homes to test out my theory!*

∝∾

INTRODUCTION

We are entering an age of higher consciousness. It may not look that way at times, as old systems struggle to maintain their hold on our minds and hearts. But business as usual has changed for good. Outmoded ways of thinking and living are going through a transformational process, due to the accelerating evolution of human consciousness.

Chaos, by necessity, precedes new birth. These changeable times demand that we know and express our authentic selves. The planetary alignments of 2011-2012, in particular, spark a revolutionary fire not seen since the 1960s. The seeds of change planted then are sprouting now. We see this in the rise of feminine power, as women ascend to leadership roles. The Divine Feminine is arising from centuries of suppression, to take her rightful place next to the Divine Masculine. As the right and left hemispheres of our brains come into balance, intuition becomes as valuable as logic in safely guiding our paths.

More than ever before, we need peace and tranquility in our homes. Our living space grounds us. If it is cluttered or inharmonious, we'll have trouble navigating the currents of change. It is my hope that the system outlined in this book helps you create stability and flow within and without—and find your higher ground.

1 MAKE YOUR HOME A SACRED SPACE

Does your home honor the sacred within you? Or is it a collection of random objects that serve a purpose but fail to nourish your soul? Perhaps it contains things you love, but over the years, has become a maze of clutter, congested with relics from the past. Our intentions to clean, clear and reorganize often get overshadowed by life's demands.

In this book you'll learn a simple method of blessing your home that turns it into a sacred space. As you work my **Astro Feng Shui** system, you'll transform every area of your home one step at a time. Each month, you'll manifest business and personal goals that previously eluded you, and deepen your self-understanding.

Feng Shui is the art of placement—purposefully arranging one's environment to create a flow of ch'i (energy) and well being. A home radiates the energetic vibe of those who live there. If you are creative and joyful, your home will reflect that. If you are often angry or depressed, your home will have a dull or stagnant energy, regardless of how nicely you arrange it. We've all seen picture-perfect homes that felt devoid of soul. And, even if the furniture is a bit shabby, some homes simply radiate openness and love. The idea is to be at home in your home, able to breathe deeply and relax—whether you live in an apartment, a trailer or a mansion.

Your home's exterior also reflects your state of mind and heart. There's a house down the street that I pass each day on my walk. Once lovely, it has fallen into disrepair and weeds surround it. Perhaps the owner has given up on life. However, by nurturing his surroundings with a little loving care, he would go a long way toward mending whatever ails him.

MY FENG SHUI INITIATION

When Feng Shui expert Sally Adams helped me revitalize my home in the summer of 2007, it ignited a passion that had me buzzing for weeks. I scrubbed, painted furniture, rearranged and tossed stuff out. I bought new sheets and a bedspread in a seductive shade of deep rose (and ultimately, a brand new bed), dug up dead plants in the backyard and purchased new potted palms for my deck. I felt the energy in my home shift with each phase of clearing, cleaning and renewing. My business improved, and an encounter at the grocery store turned into a life-changing relationship. The ch'i was flowing in my home and life due to *good Feng Shui*.

Bad Feng Shui is also easy to recognize. When I was ten, I visited a friend's house whose family lived with debris—including smelly dog hair and unwashed clothing. Fleas attacked my ankles as I waded through junk on my way to the dining room. During lunch, my friend's mother decided she'd had enough of her peanut butter and jelly sandwich—and casually tossed it over her shoulder. I knew nothing about ch'i when I was ten, but I knew I had to get out of that house! And later, I learned of the severe financial and emotional problems my friend's family was facing.

Chances are your house—and your life—aren't that bad. But you'd be surprised how even seemingly minor details such as a dying plant, a closet full of clothes you never wear or a broken copy machine can adversely affect your state of mind. And, where our thoughts go, our energy flows—or stagnates.

The Feng Shui maxim is, **"As without, so within."** The objects in your home reflect your internal state of being. Our environment is always speaking to us. Becoming conscious of your surroundings gives you clues about the habitual patterns of thought that create your reality—and helps you alter them. For example, a bunch of random stuff in your relationship corner suggests you haven't been paying much attention to your love life. Maybe that's okay for now—you're mourning a lost love or focused on your career. But once you're ready for a little romance, open your heart, clear out the clutter, add some pink, festive items and you'll be amazed what happens!

**The Feng Shui maxim is:
"As without, so within."**

For instance, a friend was embarrassed to discover that a mountain of dirty laundry had piled up in his Love gua. This had happened while he was grieving a relationship. He cleared out that corner of his bedroom, placed two red candles on a table in that gua and vowed to "clean up" his love life. Soon after, he met someone new—with whom he has formed a solid bond.

WESTERN FENG SHUI VS. TRADITIONAL

Traditional Chinese Feng Shui combines Chinese Astrology with compass directions to determine the best placements for objects such as the bed or desk. While this system is valid, I prefer Western Feng Shui, a more user-friendly system which emphasizes the "Bagua"—an octagonal map that corresponds to your floor plan. The nine basic "guas," or areas of life, fall into different sectors of the home. We'll learn more about the Bagua map in the next chapter.

The guas are sensitive to neglect and require regular maintenance. It's easy to let papers pile up on your desk, or allow dust to collect on bookshelves. Things that don't belong can also block the flow of energy. A swinging hammock that partially blocked one client's front door was symbolically keeping people away. Once she moved it, her career opened up. A stagnant pond in another person's Wealth gua was blocking her financial flow.

We must learn to hear what our environment is saying to us, to pay attention to subtle energies. You may not believe that making changes to your home can actually trigger changes in your life—until you try it. You'll feel the energy shift right away. For instance, an important Feng Shui maxim says that you should never place your office chair (or any chair) so that your back is to the door. Subconsciously, you'll feel vulnerable, open to attack. Switch the desk and chair around so that you can easily see anyone who enters, and you'll feel safer and more centered in your power.

TOXIC STUMBLING BLOCKS

Environmental toxins can undo your best efforts at creating change. If you live beneath high-voltage lines that sap your energy night and day, or your environment is polluted with cigarette smoke, even the best Feng Shui cures may not make much difference. The same goes for a leaky furnace or moldy walls that are affecting your health. If you have a chronic problem like this, you must eliminate it—or relocate, if there is no other solution.

> **If you live beneath high-voltage lines that sap your energy night and day, or your environment is polluted with cigarette smoke, even the best Feng Shui cures may not make much difference.**

It is also possible to block your results with negative thinking— refusing to recognize or accept positive developments. Feng Shui can bring about uncanny changes—regardless of whether you believe in it or not. I've had skeptics and neophytes alike try out my system, with amazing results. However, if you have persistent, unhealed psychological wounds, they can sometimes override your most determined Feng Shui efforts. Professional counseling might be needed.

If you're terrified of change—even the good kind—you may resist shifting the energy, and quickly revert to what's familiar because the positive results feel uncomfortable. If, for example, you've Feng Shui'd your Love gua and are still attracting losers, there is a deeper problem that needs to be addressed. In a case like this, Feng Shui combined with deep soul-searching and/or therapy is your route to a healthy relationship.

Sometimes, however, a stuck condition is teaching you something valuable, and in that case you're wise to not rush in and try to fix it. If you've used Feng Shui with imagination and intent, addressed your inner issues, and you're still not getting the result you want, it may be best to relax and accept things as they are for now. Perhaps the slow-moving planets have to aspect your natal chart before your reward comes through.

Or, there may be something else you're meant to do. For example, during the time Rhonda's aging, abusive mother was ill, she prayed for the end to come and set them both free. It didn't happen. Rather than receiving her inheritance, Rhonda was forced to build her career while taking care of her mother. Rhonda's perseverance paid off, though, once she surrendered to the reality of the situation.

CONQUERING CLUTTER

Clutter is a prime Feng Shui obstacle. If you've got a lot of it, look at where things pile up. These areas of your home are related to parts of your life where you have difficulty letting go of the past (we'll be looking at this next via the Bagua map). The fear of change is why so many people have a problem with clutter. They form attachments to things—even random, meaningless ones like old newspapers or grocery lists—and can't bear to throw them out. I often see this kind of attachment in the charts of those with prominent Taurus planets. It's a security issue. Being surrounded by a collection of objects makes earthy types feel protected and safe.

If clutter is your bugaboo, be gentle with yourself. Release a little bit at a time, to avoid magnifying your fear of change. Small efforts in the right direction are better than all-out campaigns that end in overwhelm and giving up. My Astro Feng Shui system will help you address each part of your home, one step at a time.

The fear of change is why so many people have a problem with clutter.

In your clutter-clearing process, ask yourself three questions about each item. If it meets at least two of the following criteria, allow it to stay. If not, let it go. Someone else will probably be thrilled to get that jade elephant lamp or myrtle-wood bread box, and you'll feel much lighter and freer.

• Do I use it?

• Is it beautiful?

• Do I love it?

If you still can't decide, clutter-clearing experts advise banishing the "maybes" to your storage shed for a year. Then, take them out and review them. The ones you didn't miss don't belong in your life. On the other hand, if you missed something a great deal, welcome it back with open arms.

ADDING ASTROLOGY TO THE MIX

My system couples Western Feng Shui with Western Astrology, whose guiding maxim is **"As above, so below."** The celestial map mirrors your inner nature and timing on earth. The horoscope, or map of the constellations, is divided into 12 sectors, or signs (Aries through Pisces), which correspond with the Bagua map and the different parts of your living space. (It's no accident that someone like me, with four planets in Cancer, sign of the home, came up with this system!)

This book will help you harness the powerful energies of your planets to catalyze meaningful change in your life. In particular, we'll be working with the New Moon, when the Moon is dark or invisible. This is the time each month when

the Sun (masculine) and Moon (feminine) join in the heavens. As in conception, it's a time in which new seeds are planted that will bear fruit over time. Each New Moon relates to a different sector of the Bagua. During the New Moon part of the 28 day cycle, set your intention, do ritual, take action and gain awareness related to the part of your life that's been activated (i.e. career, love or health). Then, as the Full Moon approaches, the results of your efforts and intentions become manifest.

> **Western astrology's guiding maxim is "As above, so below."**

GETTING CREATIVE WITH RITUAL

Let's say, for example, that your Wealth gua is about to be activated by the upcoming New Moon in Taurus. You'd perform a ritual in the far left hand corner of your home (corresponding to the Wealth gua), to align your intentions with the cosmic flow and open yourself to money-making opportunities. Maybe you'd print out a picture of Lakshmi that you found on the Net, frame and hang it in that gua. Saying prayers to the Hindu goddess of abundance during a prosperity cycle doubles your chances of receiving more wealth and well being (abundance comes in many forms, not just money).

Often people feel overwhelmed after a Feng Shui assessment of their home—so much work to do! (Most folks aren't willing to tackle it all at once the way I did). This system breaks it down into bite-sized chunks you can easily handle, which makes turning your home into a sacred space a joyful process. Working with a different part of the home each month—and witnessing the life-enhancing results—keeps your ch'i from stagnating, and reminds you that we live in a sacred universe. And, doing monthly rituals and cleansings to enhance specific parts of your life elevates your consciousness—while it keeps your home neat and clean!

ASTROLOGY AND FENG SHUI: A GOOD MATCH

Astrology and Feng Shui share a common understanding, recently confirmed by quantum physics: Life is a hologram, in which each part reflects the whole. To change our lives, we must change our thoughts—as well as our surroundings, which reflect our thoughts. **It all boils down to setting intentions.** As one of my research participants put it, "It's puzzling to me that something this innocuous could be so powerful, but it proves itself month in and month out. I think it's directly tied to intention—what we intend and believe will happen, happens. Each time it works, your intention gets stronger because you have convinced yourself what you're doing is having an effect. That's the great thing about it—the effect intensifies as time goes by because you see that it works."

Since I developed this system in 2008, I've played with different ways of combining Astrology and Feng Shui, experimenting on myself and willing friends and clients. Because I'm a Cancer, ruled by the ephemeral Moon, my home is in constant flux. I regularly move things around, adding little touches – a fresh green plant here, a new treasure map (vision board) there. **You don't have to wait for the New Moon to make changes to your environment.** Each time I hear a juicy new Feng Shui tip, I fly into action. A pink rose quartz heart in my Love gua to enhance relations. Nine red ribbons on my modem cord to bring more business via the Internet. Inevitably, good intentions create good results.

> To change our lives, we must change our thoughts—as well as our surroundings, which reflect our thoughts. It all boils down to setting intentions.

TIMING ACTIVITIES BY THE MOON

I also use the Moon's progress through the signs each month to spur home-related changes. For example, the Moon was in the earthy, nature-loving sign of Taurus the day I bought a gorgeous new plant for my Knowledge gua, which helped clear my mind and jump-started the writing of this book. I also picked up three bags of potting soil that day, to fill in the uneven spaces between the stepping stones that lead to my house (thus symbolically putting my career on more stable ground).

You can get a daily planner that shows the Moon's progress through the heavens (*www.Llewellyn.com* makes a good one), which will help put you in sync with the lunar cycle. First, it's important to understand the basic attributes shared by the signs. Signs are grouped by element. And, the signs in each element—fire, earth, air and water—have many things in common.

THE MOON BY ELEMENT

Fire signs (Aries, Leo, Sagittarius) are high energy. When the Moon is in those signs, you should have enough enthusiasm to accomplish a great deal. However, you may also be inclined to put tasks aside and go out and have a good time! The solution is to keep things fun by playing your favorite music as you work or going out for pizza with friends afterwards.

Earth signs (Taurus, Virgo, Capricorn) are steadfast. When the Moon is in those signs, you'll be able to see tasks through to the end. And, whatever you initiate now will have long-lasting results. Things move slowly when the Moon is in earth signs, though, so allow more time than you think you'll need. And, promise yourself a pleasurable reward at the end of a job well done—such as a massage, a visit to the park or a splurge on a new outfit.

Air signs (Gemini, Libra, Aquarius) are social and tend toward distraction. When the Moon is in these airy signs, it may be best to take frequent breaks. Writing projects should flow well. With tasks, invite friends or family to join you to get more done. Choose people who are full of good ideas or good conversationalists, to avoid getting bored or distracted.

Water signs (Cancer, Scorpio, Pisces) are introspective and retentive. When the Moon is in these watery signs, it's best to do tasks that have meaning for you, which help you release the past or that make you feel nourished. Work meditatively by yourself or with a family member whose company you enjoy. Choose someone who is good at letting things go.

THE MOON BY SIGN

The Moon stays in each sign for two and a half days. During that time, the prevailing vibe (what's "in the air") tends to resonate with the qualities of that sign. This reference guide suggests productive activities that are likely to flow well when the Moon passes through that particular arena of life.

Aries: Sign of pioneering efforts, fresh starts and active, athletic endeavors. Things to do: Scrub the floor, update sports equipment, attend a game or go on a hike.

Taurus: Sign of wealth, stability and sensual pleasure. Things to do: Buy or water plants, weed the garden, balance your checking account, build shelves, have a massage, fix a special meal.

Gemini: Sign of communication, writing and short trips. Things to do: Organize papers and your desk, clean and organize bookcases, buy a computer, answer emails.

Cancer: Sign of home, family, food and feelings. Things to do: Clean the refrigerator, polish or frame family pictures, buy cookware, make a nourishing meal.

Leo: Sign of pride, creativity, originality and children. Things to do: Buy festive and elegant décor, clean the kids' room, do an art project, groom the dog or cat, rehearse your monologue or attend the theater.

Virgo: Sign of work, health, details and cleanliness. Things to do: Organize files, buy herbs and health food, vacuum carpets, apply for or begin a job.

Libra: Sign of balance, fairness, marriage and love. Things to do: Put out new candles, buy a new bedspread, have a romantic date, get engaged or married, or attend a wedding.

Scorpio: Sign of wealth, transformation and commitment. Things to do: Pay your debts, become a benefactor or make a loan, make investments, have a garage sale.

Sagittarius: Sign of travel, education and adventure. Things to do: Go camping, give away books, plan or undertake a long-distance journey, sign up for or begin classes.

Capricorn: Sign of business, practicality and structure. Things to do: Build a fence, paint the deck, weed out your portfolio, start a business or new job.

Aquarius: Sign of technology, friends and progressive causes. Things to do: Clean and back up computers, host a gathering, network in new circles.

Pisces: Sign of spirituality, flowing water and charity. Things to do: Clean the pool or go swimming, go to church, volunteer your time or visit an ailing pal or family member.

As you grow accustomed to following the lunar cycle, you will see which activities naturally flow for you when the Moon is in each sign. When the Moon is in the same sign as your Sun, your core energy will be emphasized.

For example, fire signs will be more outgoing and color-ful when the Moon is in Aries, Leo or Sagittarius, while air signs will be more social and full of ideas when the Moon is in Gemini, Libra and Aquarius. Earth signs will feel especial-ly practical and results-oriented when the Moon is in Taurus, Virgo and Capricorn, while water signs may feel more intro-spective or emotional when the Moon is in Cancer, Scorpio and Pisces.

> **When the Moon is in the same sign as your Sun, your core energy will be emphasized.**

2 WORKING THE SYSTEM

I made the connection between Astrology and Feng Shui when a friend gave me a dinette set at the New Moon in my natal eleventh house (which relates to Aquarius). I placed the table and chairs in my Helpful People gua, which happened to be my kitchen. And, synchronistically, for several weeks people called with unsolicited offers of assistance. Aquarius and Helpful People go hand-in-hand, as they both relate to friends and groups—I felt like I'd tapped in to a mother lode of helpfulness.

Then I wondered if other people might get similar results by working targeted guas of their homes at astrologically-related times. So, I devised a research project – thirty people performed New Moon rituals in specific guas of their homes each month for a year. All were amazed by the results! Now I've simplified the system so anyone can use it, whether or not you know your natal chart. And, my clients and I continue to get powerful results. If you are familiar with your natal chart, you can work the part of your chart that's triggered by the New Moon, for a double dose of magic! (More details on that later on.)

No matter which version of the system was used, the outcomes were fascinating—one participant spiffed up her bathroom in the Creativity gua at the appropriate time, and won $3500 at a local casino. Another built a new support structure under his kitchen sink (in his Family gua), and his relationship with his mother improved. Some rituals triggered unsettling changes that ultimately proved beneficial—after a ritual at the New Moon eclipse (eclipses are especially powerful), one woman realized her marriage was over. Yet breaking free from her husband has opened a more fulfilling path for her.

To spark your imagination, I'll be sharing creative examples of how my clients, research participants and I have worked the Astro Feng Shui system. But first, let's determine which part of your home to activate each month at the New Moon. (If you don't have a calendar that notes the New Moons, refer to the table at the back of this book and mark the New Moons for the entire year on your wall or desk calendar).

> One participant spiffed up her bathroom
> in the Creativity gua at the appropriate
> time, and won $3500 at a local casino.

THE NINE GUAS

Next we'll look at the Bagua map. "Ba" means "eight," and the "guas" represent different sections of the home. The Bagua's eight sides plus the middle section make up the nine major aspects of life—Career, Knowledge, Family, Prosperity, Fame, Love, Creativity, Helpful People and Health. Each gua relates to an astrological sign (because there are nine guas and twelve signs, some of the signs correlate to more than one gua).

Here's a quick rundown on the guas, signs and houses:

Career and Life Path Gua: In the area near your front door, you open out to the world and make your mark in life. Like the Ascendant in the natal chart, it shows how you appear to others, plus your image and physical body. It also relates to your career expression. Known as the "mouth of ch'i," this gua correlates with the sign of Aries.

Prosperity Gua: In this area, the far left corner of your home, you seek wealth on every level, including money. One of the power areas of the home, this gua correlates with gratitude. Being thankful is the secret to loving what you have, and enables you to have more. The Wealth gua is associated with the signs of Taurus.

Knowledge Gua: In this area, you expand your horizons through training, travel and spiritual studies. Making improvements to this gua helps clear your mind and improve communication with others. This gua correlates with the signs of Gemini and Sagittarius.

Family Gua: Here you gain emotional satisfaction by having a comfortable home, enough money to pay the bills, and healthy family connections. If something is amiss in your family life, look to this gua – which is associated with the sign of Cancer.

Creativity and Children Gua: This is where you cultivate more fun and creativity, and improve relations with children—yours or others peoples'. This gua is also associated with gambling and speculation, and it correlates with the sign of Leo.

Health Gua: This area at the center of the Bagua and home is the well from which all else springs, as it touches every other gua. It is associated with physical, mental and spiritual health as well as habit patterns, the signs of Virgo and Pisces.

Love Gua: Another power corner of the Bagua, this area at the far right corner of your home is associated with all relationships, not just the romantic variety. This includes the relationship with yourself, as well as clients, agents, lawyers and business partners. This gua links with the sign of Libra.

Fame Gua: Here is where you grow your reputation, gain publicity and become recognized for your contributions, especially those in your career. This gua also shows your integrity (or lack thereof), and is associated with the sign of Capricorn.

Helpful People Gua: This is where you receive aid and blessings, from those on Earth as well as the angelic realms. This includes those you already know, as well as those you need to attract to help you fulfill your needs. This gua is associated with the sign of Aquarius.

THE BAGUA MAP

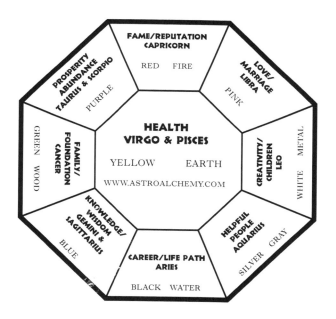

Note: The correlations between the signs and guas on the Bagua map show you the area of your home to work at each New Moon. Dates and times of the New Moons through 2020 are listed in the appendix. Or, check your astrological daily planner or an online ephemeris such as *www.zodiacal.com.*

Let's say the upcoming New Moon is in the sign of Libra. Libra corresponds to the Love gua, as shown in the diagram of the Bagua. Thus, the part of your home that falls in the Love gua is the area you'll be working at the Libra New Moon. For specific tips on maximizing the Love gua, read the chapter on the New Moon in Libra.

ASSESS YOUR GUAS

It's a good idea to assess each area of your life and related areas of your home ahead of time. Jot down some notes about improvements you'd like to see over the next 12 months. If you have specific goals, like painting the bathroom for company coming in December, time the painting job to correspond with the related New Moon (if the bathroom is in your Family gua, target the Cancer New Moon). Or, let's say you want to start teaching a series of classes. If you set your intention and/or launch the classes at the New Moon in Gemini or Sagittarius, the signs of teaching and learning, they'll have cosmic momentum behind them.

You can also write down personal goals, such as manifesting a new relationship or getting your fallen fitness regimen back on track. Look for the New Moons that correspond to these areas of life to activate your goals.

If you want to launch a business, for instance, time that new beginning to correspond to the New Moon in Aries (the Career and Life Path gua) or Capricorn (the Fame gua) and you'll be more likely to succeed. Or, if you can't wait for a particular New Moon to roll around, begin your project during the time of the month when the Moon is in the appropriate sign (see the Moon guide in the previous chapter), preferably at a New Moon. For something as important as a business launch, home purchase or marriage, however, you'd be wise to consult an astrologer to make sure that significant planets aren't retrograde, and other cycles to your chart are aligned what you're planning.

If you want to launch a business, time it to correspond to the New Moon in Aries.

SKETCH OUT YOUR FLOOR PLAN

Next, make a sketch of your floor plan, roughly the same size as the Bagua map. Include any attached outside areas such as a garage or patio. Then, lay this sketch on top of the Bagua to determine where your guas are located. If you live in a multi-story house, repeat this process for each level (you can perform your ritual on both levels or only one). The guas merge fluidly into one another, so don't worry about dividing your home exactly. Trace a rough diagram of the nine guas onto the sketch of your home, and label each one according to its function. If your room, apartment or office is part of a larger home or complex, just overlay the Bagua map onto your individual space rather than trying to map the entire structure.

For most, overlaying the Bagua onto the home is simple. The Career gua, for instance, usually corresponds to the front door (this can be the front door to the entire home or the entrance to a single room, if you rent a room in a house.) But what happens if your front entrance is not in the center of the wall—or is recessed, creating a missing chunk in the Bagua? The following examples can help you figure out what to do.

Example One – Missing Piece from Helpful People Gua

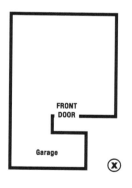

This house has an attached garage in front. The Helpful People gua is missing, and the front door is located at the end of a garden path, behind the garage. James and Paula, the couple who live here, were struggling with their careers; neither felt adequately supported by their community. We placed a potted plant at the empty corner (marked by an X), to symbolically fill in the missing chunk. You could also bury a crystal, plant a prayer flag on a pole or put a fountain here—anything that feels right, to complete the Bagua. The front door itself was dark and uninviting, and on top of that, the door bell didn't work! (Symbolically, clients couldn't get through).

James cleaned the area and Paula hung a bamboo wind chime above the door to get the ch'i flowing, which resulted in a career boost for both. However, the bell was not fixed, nor was the door repainted. This came back to haunt the couple later, when tough Saturn cycles hit both their charts and they faced foreclosure on their home. I reminded them about the cures left undone. At the New Moon that triggered her Career gua, Paula spearheaded the changes to the front door. She also added a money plant to the master bathroom, or Wealth gua, where it would be reflected in two sets of mirrors to amplify its wealth-enhancing qualities. By the Full Moon two weeks later, both James and Paula had found new positions and money was flowing in.

> **The doorbell didn't work - symbolically, clients couldn't get through.**

Example Two – Missing Pieces from Fame and Love Gua

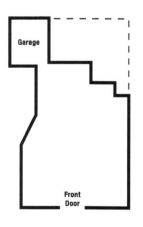

In this example, both the Fame and Love gua are missing a chunk in the backyard area of the home. Tish lives here with her 16-year-old son. She is a painter and an Expressive Arts Therapist who's building her practice and gaining a reputation in the community. At the New Moon in her Fame gua, Tish (with a little help from her son) focused on the back yard—sweeping, clearing and pulling weeds, and cleaning the patio table. To affirm her success in the Expressive Arts Therapy field, she painted an antique door with whimsical flowers (imagining the seeds she has planted will sprout and bloom) in shades of red and purple, and leaned it against the back wall in her Fame gua.

Results came fast. Tish and a friend found a terrific studio space and submitted a rental application. "My big dream is to have a center," she said, "and this space was almost perfect." The landlord rented to someone else, however, and Tish was crestfallen. Once she got past her disappointment, though, she realized that this experience had given new life to her dream. Also, the same week she met someone at a local street fair who loved her paintings—and wrote a feature about her work in an online newspaper. (Don't get discouraged if initial possibilities don't pan out—it took Tish another year to find the space that was meant for her.)

PREPARATION FOR YOUR RITUAL

A ritual can be simple or complex. In her fun and inspirational book, *Move Your Stuff, Change Your Life*, Karen Rauch Carter tells the story of a woman who, upon first learning about Feng Shui, walked over to her Love gua and tossed a pair of red panties in the corner, saying "There, take that!" Soon, claims Rauch, the woman was happily married to a millionaire. You might prefer to do an elaborate ritual with pink candles, special incense and love incantations. Whatever works! Remember, it's all about the power of your intention—the thoughts you're holding about what you desire. I'll suggest rituals for each New Moon, to help you align your subconscious mind with your conscious intentions and super-conscious mind (the part of you which connects to higher realms of existence).

Karen Rauch Carter tells the story of a woman who, upon first learning about Feng Shui, walked over to her Love gua and tossed a pair of red panties in the corner, saying "There, take that!" Soon, claims Rauch, the woman was happily married to a millionaire.

To prepare for your New Moon blessing ceremony, perform the following steps. You can do this part in advance of the New Moon:

Assess the gua you're going to activate. How does the energy feel? Is it heavy and stuck, or light and free? Remove any objects that don't need to be there or are cluttering up the space. Banish anything that's broken or dying—like plants that have seen better days. The gua must feel as sacred and serene as possible—even if it's the laundry room!

Perform a thorough cleansing. Remove all dust, dirt and cobwebs. Scrub the floor or countertops. Clap your hands, shake a rattle, burn sage or incense, toss salt in the corners or spray an aromatherapy mist in the air to disperse any stagnant energy.

Add appropriate elements and colors. Consult the guide that follows. Balance the five elements—wood, earth, metal, fire and water—by placing them in the area where they best resonate. Water, for instance, nourishes Career—so it's good to put a fountain near your front door. Metal is destructive in Family (so nix the sword collection in that gua). Plants are great, as the Family color is green, but you'd want to avoid the color white, associated with metal. The Creative and Destructive cycles of elements are shown in the accompanying charts. If this seems too complex, just work with the colors at first. Once you feel more harmony in your environment, you can experiment with deeper energetic change.

Add enhancements. Also known as "cures," these are objects that open and harmonize space. Classic cures include mirrors, wind chimes, crystals, and lamps. See the chart below for specific ideas. Be sure to purchase candles and other items for your ritual.

The gua must feel as sacred and serene as possible—even if it's the laundry room!

DO A HOUSE BLESSING AND CLEARING

If your house contains a great deal of stagnant energy, you may wish to do a cleansing of the entire premises to clear the psychic space before doing your New Moon rituals. This is particularly important if you've just changed residences, or if someone has recently moved out or passed away. Also, if you've had a fight or other unpleasant encounter with someone, clearing the space can help you start fresh and reclaim your peace of mind.

A house cleansing is also useful if you are buying or selling a home. Before you move into a new house, clear the energy of the former inhabitants. And, if you want to sell your home, cleansing the space will make it more appealing to prospective buyers.

I gave the following cleansing ritual to a client who was facing foreclosure on her rental property. She'd had to evict the former tenant, who had turned out to be a drug dealer, and his negative energy still polluted the environment. No one wanted to rent the place. She performed the ritual, and rented the condo that weekend to a great couple.

You can also bless a space if you're there for a short time. While caretaking some children while their parents were on a business trip, Grace decided to cleanse the heaviness in the air. (She knew the couple had had bitter fights in the house, and that their long-time canine companion had recently passed). Grace spritzed each corner of the house with a spray bottle of water, praying that anything that was no longer for the highest good of the family would leave. Then she carried a lit candle around the space and declared, "Let there be light!" Interestingly, when the couple returned, the man said, "It feels like a white tornado has been through here!"

Cleansings are powerful. It's best to keep yours simple, however, especially if you have never done this before. Here's what I recommend:

- Begin at the entrance to your home or office. Say a short prayer, asking helpful deities or spirits to aid you in cleansing the space.
- Slowly walk clockwise through every corner of the home, clapping your hands loudly while commanding negative energies to leave. Simply repeat, "Cleansing, banishing, clearing this space."
- Light a stick of sage or incense, and repeat the process, as you call in positive and harmonious energies. Say, "Blessing this space and all who enter it. Only helpful energies are allowed in now."
- Give thanks for the help you've been given. You may also cleanse and bless outside areas in the same way if they seem to require it.

If you want to sell your home, cleansing the space will make it more appealing to prospective buyers.

CREATE AN ALTAR

An altar is a sacred space containing objects which hold special meaning. Many of us, especially women, instinctively create altars throughout our homes. For example, perhaps the top of your piano features Grandma's picture with a vase of flowers next to it, on a doily that belonged to her. Altars keep us connected to who and what we love.

I have an ancestor altar in the terrarium above my dining table (Family gua), featuring pictures of my ancestors and other symbolic items. My personal altar, where I pray each morning, is the bureau in my bedroom (Love gua). It features items that represent the four elements, symbolizing balance and wholeness: A jar of water from sacred lakes around the world, two pink candles that I light each morning and a jar of earth from Philae, the Egyptian island sacred to Isis. To bring in the air element, I open the nearby window. My personal altar also contains a carving of Isis and Osiris, bobcat and goat skulls (two of my totems) and assorted power objects.

At each New Moon, it's good to create a small altar in the gua you are working, with items related to that gua. For example, a Health altar might contain a bowl of lemons, vase of yellow flowers and a yellow candle.

Altars keep us connected to who and what we love.

Attributes and Enhancements

The following table is based on the creative and destructive cycles of the five elements. It's good to emphasize the elements and related colors that strengthen each gua, and minimize those that weaken it. (Some guas are more strongly associated with colors than elements, so they have no restrictions on which elements to use).

Water nourishes wood but puts out fire. Therefore, water elements enhance the Career (water) and Family (wood) guas, but weaken the Fame (fire) gua. This is why fountains are good in the Career gua but not in Fame. And, earth muddies water but produces metal, so earth tones are less favorable in Career and better suited to Health or Creativity. If you find this information confusing, just use your intuition—and see what works for you!

Aries - Career and Life Path: Identity, image, work, body, path in life
Attributes: Water, black, dark colors, metal, round shapes
Elements to minimize: Earth, yellow, fire, red, square, pointed shapes
Enhancements: Wind chimes, fountain, two evergreen plants, heavy statues

Taurus - Prosperity: Finances, self-esteem, values, priorities
Attributes: Blue, purple, red, gold, green
Enhancements: Fish tank, jade plant, gold coins, treasure box, a picture of Lakshmi, goddess of wealth

Gemini - Knowledge: Research, travel, teaching, learning, beliefs, thoughts
Attributes: Blue, black, green.
Enhancements: Books, travel posters, desk, treasure map, bells, lamps

Cancer - Family: Family, home, ancestry, foundation, emotional well-being
Attributes: Wood, blue, green, rectangles, columns
Elements to minimize: Metal, white, round shapes
Enhancements: Family pictures, green candles and plants, prized heirlooms.

Leo - Creativity: Art, children, romance, joy, gambling, playfulness
Attributes: Metal, earth, white, pastel, round, square shapes
Elements to minimize: Fire, red, pointed shapes
Enhancements: Crystals, original artwork, pictures of kids or baby animals

Virgo - Physical Health: Health, habits, service, jobs, volunteer work
Attributes: Earth, yellow, red, fire, square, pointed shapes
Elements to minimize: Wood, green, columns
Enhancements: Yellow flowers, salt lamp, bowl of lemons, statue of Kuan Yin, goddess of compassion

Libra - Love and Marriage: Marriage, business partners, self-love
Attributes: Red, pink, white, lilac, peach
Enhancements: Two crystal rabbits, pink candles, matching end tables/lamps

Scorpio - Prosperity: Shared finances, commitments, transformation
Attributes: Blue, green, purple, red, gold
Enhancements: Fish tank, jade plant, gold coins, treasure box, picture of Ganesh, god of transformation

Sagittarius - Knowledge: Travel, speaking, publishing, philosophizing
Attributes: Blue, green, black
Enhancements: Books, travel posters, desk, treasure map, bells, lamps

Capricorn - Fame: Calling in life, reputation, business, status
Attributes: Fire, red, wood, green, triangular, pointed shapes
Elements to minimize: Water, black
Enhancements: Framed certificates, BBQ, fireplace, red candles, plants

Aquarius - Helpful People: Community, friends, hopes, social causes
Attributes: White, gray, black, silver
Enhancements: Silver box, pictures of angels, dining table, mirrors

Pisces - Spiritual Health: Spiritual and mental health, rest, rejuvenation
Attributes: Earth, yellow, red, fire, square, pointed shapes
Elements to Avoid: Wood, green, columns
Enhancements: Yellow flowers, Kuan Yin statue, salt lamp, bowl of lemons

CREATIVE AND DESTRUCTIVE CYCLE OF ELEMENTS

CREATIVE CYCLE

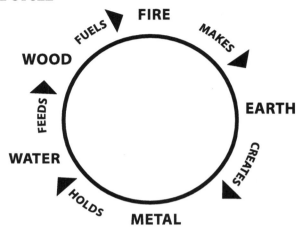

DESTRUCTIVE CYCLE

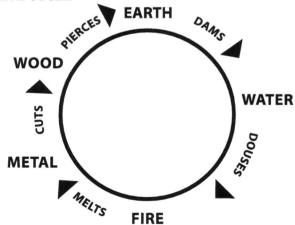

AT THE NEW MOON

The New Moon (or dark Moon) is a potent time, especially in the waxing period 12 hours prior to the Sun and Moon uniting in the same sign. Your ritual will be most effective when performed in this waxing phase, but anytime in the 24 hour period before or after the New Moon works. If the exact union of Sun and Moon should happen at 2 a.m., there's no need to stay up until then to perform your ritual—just do it before you go to bed. Likewise, if the New Moon happens at 2 p.m. while you're at work, simply do your ritual that morning or when you come home in the evening.

You can also do your ritual at any point during the two weeks leading up to the Full Moon. It may not be as powerful as it would have been at the union of the Sun and Moon, but you'll still be within the correct astrological energy for whatever gua you're working or result you're looking for.

> If the New Moon happens at 2 p.m. while you're at work, simply do your ritual that morning or when you come home in the evening.

Here's a typical New Moon process:

- **Set your intentions.** Word them as if they'd already happened. If the New Moon is in Cancer, for example, write down your intention for increased family harmony. "I give thanks that my mother and I are on good terms and easily express love and affection to each other."

- **Sit or stand quietly in the gua at hand.** Center yourself and breathe deeply; feel a connection to the Divine. Bless your sacred space. Light a candle in the color of that gua. Call on your guides, favorite deities and ancestors to help you realize your goal. Speak your intention out loud, then place the paper on which you've written it under the candle.

- **Give thanks that the goal is already yours.** Enjoy the feeling of serenity you've generated. Blow out the candle, unless you plan to let it burn down. (Never leave a candle unattended, unless it's enclosed).

- **Pay attention to any dreams or intuitive promptings during the following days and weeks.** You may feel inspired to take some action, like sending your mother a letter of gratitude, or calling someone to assist you with a goal. Be sure to follow through.

- **Watch for results.** It may always not come in the form you intended, but there will be a manifestation associated with the gua you activated, often near the Full Moon two weeks later (which brings the New Moon cycle to fruition). Occasionally there will be a seemingly negative result or loss, which is necessary to improve conditions in the area of life you've been working.

> **It may not always come in the form you intended, but there will be a manifestation associated with the gua you activated.**

IF YOU KNOW YOUR NATAL CHART

For even greater results, you can also perform a New Moon ritual according to your natal chart, if you're familiar with it (or, consult an astrologer to find out which house of your chart is being activated). Simply look to the house where the New Moon falls, and work the corresponding gua.

- New Moon in the first house – Career and Life Purpose gua

- New Moon in the second house – Prosperity gua
- New Moon in the third house – Knowledge gua
- New Moon in the fourth house – Family gua
- New Moon in the fifth house – Creativity and Children gua
- New Moon in the sixth house – Health gua
- New Moon in the seventh house – Love gua
- New Moon in the eighth house – Wealth gua
- New Moon in the ninth house – Knowledge gua
- New Moon in the tenth house – Fame gua
- New Moon in the eleventh house – Helpful People gua
- New Moon in the twelfth house – Health gua

Receiving that fateful dinette set at the New Moon in my eleventh house was the catalyst for this initial theory. Aligning the house of the natal chart with the physical home made sense to me. And, this method got results. First-house rituals sparked physical and career transformations in a number of peoples' lives. Fourth house rituals helped shift the status quo in family relationships. And eighth house rituals yielded wealth, often unexpectedly. If trying this method intrigues you, feel free to explore it in addition to the basic system that's outlined in this book.

3 NEW MOON IN ARIES AND THE CAREER GUA

A baby's first cry upon meeting the world. A thoroughbred's bolt from the starting gate. The New Moon in Aries is your coming-out party! For the last month, as the Sun moved through dreamy Pisces, you may have felt more emotional or unfocused than usual. You might have been hiding out, doing inner work or preparing for something. Now, you're feeling restless and ready for some action!

The New Moon in Aries makes you bold. It's all about personal freedom. The first of the three fire signs, Aries is direct and spontaneous. Now you're quick to speak what's on your mind and ask for what you want—and people respond! Aries represents your physical appearance and image, along with the steps you take to promote yourself in the world. Intentions you create now can reap big results, especially in your career.

Things to do at the New Moon in Aries:
- Get a new hairstyle or buy new clothes
- Embark on a fitness or weight loss campaign
- Make new contacts to advance your career
- Take a personal development or business course
- Become more independent – go solo to a movie or dinner
- Tell somebody what you really think (politely!)
- Send out resumes or launch a website to promote yourself
- Go on job interviews

ARIES AND THE CAREER GUA

Aries correlates with the Career and Life Path gua, located in the middle of the south side of the Bagua map. This is the gua you'll be working during this New Moon cycle. Its element is water, and its color is black. For most of us, this is the area surrounding the front door, both inside and out. Make sure it is clean, clear and inviting to flow with your career and energy.

QUICK FIXES TO ENHANCE THE CAREER GUA:

- Water elements, such as fountains or fish tanks
- Undulating forms – statues, artwork, curved gardens
- Dark, rich colors such as black, mahogany, midnight blue, forest green
- A dash of red – a red ribbon on the doorknob or two red geraniums in pots
- A working, easy-to-locate doorbell
- A mirror placed at eye level
- A symbol of the career you wish to develop
- Plenty of good lighting (including a bright, cobweb-free porch-light)
- An uncluttered and stable pathway to your door
- A thick, impressive welcome mat in dark shades
- Nicely trimmed trees and shrubs

At the New Moon in Aries, it's time to clean, clear and bless your Career and Life Path gua—and set your intention to step out and express your energy and talent.

At a recent New Moon in Aries, I hung an image of an undulating waterfall next to my front door to stimulate flow. Then, on a table inside my front door I lit a red candle, and set my intentions for career success. An intriguing possibility for my web site came to me that month out of left field. Pay attention to ideas or suggestions that pop up, related to your intentions.

INSPIRING RITUALS FROM MY RESEARCH PARTICIPANTS

Jack, an Aries Sun sign, is a teacher and healer. This New Moon fell close to his birthday, giving it extra impact. He washed his front door and cleaned the glass, vacuumed the entrance and shook out the door mat. He exchanged a dried-out plant for a healthy hibiscus, and threw out or put away things lying around the door. Then he burned sage, lit a few candles and recited a Science of Mind prayer for his business.

"Since then," he reports, "I've set up my latest class, and it was so easy to do I could never have planned it to happen the way it did. I needed a web site, and my friend offered to do it for free. Also, I wanted to do more trade shows, and then met someone willing to share booth space. Amazing!"

Because Suzanne, a Sagittarian, is missing a chunk of the Bagua, her Career gua falls in her dining room rather than the front door area. Archers tend to enthusiastically start things, then tire of them and move on to more excitement. Suzanne had several projects gathering dust on the dining room table in her Career gua. Just prior to the New Moon, she cleared and blessed the area, then went out of town on a business trip. There, she took vigorous beach walks—which made her feel so great, she committed to getting more regular exercise. "This has been a real jumpstart into a new cycle," she says. "I've even signed up for a business coaching boot camp."

> **Archers tend to enthusiastically start things, then tire of them and move on to more excitement.**

Gayle, an Aquarius, redid her front porch. She got rid of plants that were struggling, moved other plants around to more favorable locations, and bought a hefty new welcome mat and an attractive bamboo screen to make the space more inviting. Then, she taped her health-related company's brochure over the inside of the front door. She wrote affirmations for business growth on 3 x 5 cards, read them aloud then left the cards on a table inside the front door for the week following her ritual. Doing this kept her intentions fresh in her mind.

Following a hunch, Gayle gave her brother, a successful businessman, a large plant that had been partially blocking her entryway. "Moving it really opened up the porch," she relates, "and reminded me of how I block my own access to success." Soon after that, in a fascinating twist, her brother began working with her—and Gayle's business tripled! (Aquarians, though bright and full of ideas, usually do best when they're part of a team).

Grace, a Virgo writer, had been directionless and unmotivated. The Aries New Moon activated the kitchen area of her small cottage, so she scrubbed her appliances, counters and floor. This brought out her Virgoan zeal for cleanliness and order, which immediately made her feel better. Then, she set up a mirror behind the stove to reflect more prosperity, and cleaned the burners (the stove is a Feng Shui wealth symbol and must always be kept clean). Soon, the entire kitchen was sparkling!

By that time, Grace was really getting into it. So she decided to blast the outside of her cottage with a power hose—removing cobwebs, mold and moss that had accumulated. She burned sage as she walked around her kitchen and outside her front door, saying affirmative prayers for renewed career inspiration. Soon after, Grace enrolled in a memoir-writing class which inspired her greatly—and now she's churning out stories, collecting them in a soon-to-be-published book.

The stove is a Feng Shui wealth symbol and must always be kept clean.

Sandy tested out my New Moon theory because it appealed to her domestic nature. With a strong emphasis in her chart on the comfort-seeking, nurturing sign of Cancer, Sandy confided that she is in love with everything related to home. Business had been slow with her small, home-based web business, so when the New Moon activated her Career and Life Purpose gua, Sandy focused on her front porch.

"It is a bit problematic," she explained, "as the dogs are always racing to the door to bark at the UPS guy, and knocking things over. I also realized I hadn't cleaned the blinds and windows since I don't know when, and the front door needed a wash-down and oil. I got to work, adding a new entrance mat and a bench in a fabulous dark green, plus I placed a water image of a heron outside."

It took all day for Sandy to complete her project. "But when finished I had solved the dog issue by allowing a space for them. I transformed the whole area and performed a New Moon blessing. Imagine my smile as part way through my work on the door area, I got a $400 order on the web. I then committed to redoing my Google ads and cleaning up my site. Now, each day brings new orders for my web-based store!"

Lydia, a psychologist with the Sun in Aries, was amazed at how much her body transformed during this New Moon cycle (remember, this gua also relates to the physical body and image). For many years she'd suffered from an intestinal disorder, trying different treatments and diets with no results. At the New Moon, Lydia swept the walkway leading to her door as well as cleaning the porch, and hung a gold bell on the door for good luck. Then, just inside the door, she lit a red candle and asked for help.

Soon, Lydia felt guided to try a gluten-free diet. Within a few months she was 15 pounds lighter and nearly symptom-free. "My whole outlook has changed," she says, "and I relate to food completely differently. My career is advancing, too—I've launched a merchant part of my website and am getting a good response."

Many of my clients have boosted their energy level and health by working the Career and Life Path gua. One found that after cleaning and clearing that gua and setting his intention for greater health, his energy level improved dramatically. "So much so," he related, "that I've been visiting the local swimming pool most mornings. And, I have achieved a personal best of 23 consecutive laps." Another client got off to a slow start with her new regimen because Mercury was retrograde at her New Moon ritual, but she still achieved results. "I felt like I was going backwards at first," she said, "but by the Full Moon I was in the groove of my new fitness and nutrition regimen. Now I have a program I can stick with, with achievable goals."

WORKING THE OPPOSITE GUA

On the Bagua map, the Fame gua is directly opposite the Career gua. They are part of an axis—enhancing one can bring results in the other. For example, business ventures you begin at the New Moon in Aries can bring you attention during the Capricorn cycle nine months later. If you're feeling industrious (or need publicity), add some red elements to your Fame gua at the New Moon. Or, hang some framed certificates to boost your reputation.

> **If you're feeling industrious (or need publicity), add some red elements to your Fame gua at the New Moon.**

SUGGESTED RITUAL FOR THE ARIES
NEW MOON:

Pump Up Your Life Force

You will need: A red candle, a goblet of water, a pen and paper.

Position your candle at a comfortable and safe spot in your Career gua. Set the goblet of water nearby. Light the candle and focus on the flame to center yourself. Take some deep breaths and consider your immediate goals for your career and/or body image. Imagine an inner Sun in your solar plexus, with a fire burning in the center of it. On the inhale, fan that fire and drop into it any negative thoughts, emotions, or images that are standing in your way from experiencing a healthy career or physical self. On the exhale, transform all that's been incinerated into light that radiates out of every pore.

Continue this breathing pattern until your thoughts and feelings have been neutralized. (If you know the Breath of Fire, which involves taking rapid breaths into your belly through your nose, you can include it). When you feel complete, bring your awareness to your heart and feel appreciation.

Dip your fingers into the goblet, and flick a little water onto your solar plexus area, to affirm your cleansing and renewal. Then, write down what you wish to achieve within the next 30-day timeframe, and set the paper next to the candle. Keep it realistic; if you shoot too high and your subconscious mind rebels, you may set yourself up for disappointment (i.e. "I now win $100 million in the lottery.")

Here are a few realistic examples: "I now welcome ten new paying clients who are greatly benefited by the services I offer." Or, "I now find the energy and resolve to embark on a healthy eating and fitness regimen."

WORKSHEET FOR THE NEW MOON IN ARIES

Gua that is activated for me at this New Moon:

_____

_____

_____

Changes I'll make or enhancements I'll add to this gua and/or its opposite:

1. _____

2. _____

3. _____

4. _____

My intentions for this month related to the New Moon theme:

1. _____

2. _____

3. _____

Results I have manifested:

_____

_____

_____

_____

4 NEW MOON IN TAURUS AND THE WEALTH GUA

Ferdinand the Bull grazing happily in his pasture. Aphrodite and her consort reveling in sacred love play. The New Moon in Taurus conjures up images of contentment and sensual pleasure. Here you learn to enjoy the physical realm and find security. When you're attuned to nature and your body wisdom, you instinctively make choices that fulfill you and affirm your worth to yourself—and others.

After the go-get-'em energy of Aries, in this cycle you settle in, claim your territory and carve out a niche for yourself. The pace is slower in this sign, giving you the opportunity to relax and smell the roses.

> **The New Moon in Taurus conjures up images of contentment and sensual pleasure.**

At the New Moon in Taurus, it's time to make a commitment to develop your talents and abilities and put them to more lucrative use. A fixed, determined sign, Taurus rules the natural world, which includes making money—preferably in an enjoyable way. Here we are reminded that money is just energy, and the more we think positive thoughts about it, the more it flows our way. Now we focus on creative pursuits, and cultivate more beauty in our lives. And, we strengthen our self-esteem so that we feel good about ourselves, no matter what our current financial, physical or romantic status may be.

Things to do at the New Moon in Taurus:
- Look in the mirror and declare what you love about yourself
- Ask for a raise or look for more rewarding work
- Develop a fun, money-making project
- Deepen your sensual connection to someone you

love
- Plant a garden, prune deadwood or buy new plants
- Take artistic or self-esteem-enhancing classes
- Put a $100 bill in your wallet to feel wealthy
- Make an investment in land or beautiful possessions
- Get a massage or beauty treatment

TAURUS AND THE WEALTH GUA

Taurus correlates with the Wealth gua, located in the far left corner from your front door. This is the gua you'll be working during this New Moon cycle. Its colors are purple, red, metallic gold and green. Make sure this area is clean, bright and free of broken items or things that symbolize lack to you in any way. Add items that make you feel wealthy.

QUICK FIXES TO ENHANCE THE WEALTH GUA

- A healthy green plant – especially a jade or lucky bamboo plant
- Silk curtains or draped fabrics in purple, red, gold or green shades
- A picture or statue of Lakshmi, or a golden Buddha
- A bowl of coins or "treasure chest" with jewelry spilling out of it
- A chunk of purple amethyst or green malachite
- A hundred dollar bill
- Images of what you want to own, with affirmations that they're yours
- Moving water, such as a fountain or fish tank
- Wind chimes

It's important to remember while in this cycle that prosperity is a state of mind. In this materialistic society, we can easily get caught up in trying to accumulate things, and feel deprived when we lack that gorgeous wardrobe, or shiny new car. Yet those with the least amount of worldly possessions can actually be the most prosperous. In India, poor people travel from all over the country to die in the sacred city of Benares. If they're able to reach this Holy Grail, they consider themselves eternally blessed with a kind of wealth that transcends this earthly plane.

It's important to remember while in this cycle that prosperity is a state of mind.

On the other hand, there are those who possess plenty of money, but live in a state of lack. My father was raised in the Depression, and he learned to hoard every nickel. Despite having plenty of money in the bank, he shops at thrift stores, and wouldn't dream of treating himself to a pleasure trip—or even a meal out. Nor does he share his resources with others, or use them to make the world a better place. Sadly, despite his apparent wealth, he lives in poverty.

The Wealth gua is sometimes called the "blessings" gua, because it symbolizes that for which we are thankful. Being grateful for even small blessings opens the doorway for more to flow in. It's good to get in the habit of affirming (preferably writing down) before bed five things that happened that day for which you are grateful—it begins to change your consciousness.

If you feel lack in a particular area of life, one way to create more flow is to give away whatever you most need. Not enough love? Find someone on whom to bestow your affections. Short on time? Give some of your valuable time to others. The same goes for money: If things are tight, break through the logjam by making a donation to your favorite cause, which affirms your trust in the ebb and flow of life. Also, focus on helping others create more wealth in their lives, and you're bound to create the same for yourself.

Being grateful for even small blessings opens the doorway for more to flow in.

Pay attention to unconscious ways in which you affirm lack. Some time ago, I felt annoyed at not having enough hangers in my closet. Putting my clothes away each day had become an exercise in frustration. This pattern was particularly insidious, as my closet was in my Wealth gua! Then one day the metaphoric light bulb went on, and I ran to the storage shed to get more hangers. Suddenly I felt a luxurious sense of expansion and ease, which made me feel wealthier. Maybe your office is in the Wealth gua, and you are constantly short of paper clips or rubber bands. Invest in a nice, big box of whatever you lack, and witness how abundant you feel!

During this New Moon a few years ago, I took a close look at my office, which occupied the corresponding gua in my previous home. Having a home office in the Wealth gua is auspicious—as long as it doesn't get overrun with papers and projects, as mine had. I began purging my files of useless, outdated info. Many of the things I'd been holding onto can be found on the Internet—so I let them go.

Then, I took everything off my desk, cleaned and rearranged it according to the Bagua (yes, even your desk can be Feng Shui'd!) I placed a beautiful treasure box I'd made for Wealth in the left hand corner, and another decorated with romantic images in the right-hand Love corner. (That was all I could do, given space limitations). I also added a new mouse pad featuring a colorful image of Ganesh, the Hindu god of blessings, to bring me prosperous energies as I work. For that month's New Moon ritual, I lit metallic gold candles and invoked for more astrology clients—a request to which the Universe rapidly responded.

Even your desk can be Feng Shui'd!

INSPIRING RITUALS FROM MY RESEARCH
PARTICIPANTS

Nancy, a Capricorn, and her husband Brian, a Taurus, were out of balance regarding finances. Nancy worked hard as a massage therapist. Brian struggled as a salesman, never making a dent in the debt load he'd accrued before their marriage. Nancy felt burdened—and I realized why when I saw their Wealth gua. There was an altar to Lakshmi, goddess of abundance—a good start. But a second female image was unrelated to wealth. With two feminine images in this gua, no wonder Nancy was carrying the load (Capricorns tend to instinctively shoulder burdens).

We removed the unrelated image and replaced it with a wooden carving of a fierce Aztec warrior. Much better! But something was still amiss—the nondescript beige curtains. The next day, I gave the couple some burgundy and gold silk shantung curtains (Wealth colors) I'd had in storage, which brightened up the space.

That night at the New Moon in Taurus (which favored both their Sun signs), Nancy and Brian lit red candles in their newly energized space and invoked greater prosperity. A week later, Brian's bank merged with another financial institution and offered to liquidate his credit card debt for a fraction of what he owed. He and Nancy were thrilled!

At the New Moon in her Wealth gua, Stephanie, a balance-loving Libra, lit a purple candle and officially opened her Tibetan bowl healing school, declaring its abundant success. "I wrote my monthly New Moon check to myself from the Universe," she related, "and placed it on my altar. And, my first advanced class for the new school is full—we are off and running!" Plus, she received an unexpected check that month from her Dad's estate. Writing herself a check was a way of partnering with the Universe to attain her goals—an appropriate Libra activity.

At the New Moon corresponding to his Wealth gua, Greg, a Virgo realtor, planted an apple and fig tree in the Wealth sector of his yard (planting is a power activity for

Virgo, which rules agriculture). He also hooked up a fountain, and planted arugula and mint around the driveway. Inside, he cleaned the bookcase in that gua, threw out old magazines and gave some books away. He relates that since then, doors have miraculously opened. And, the fig tree is bearing fruit—along with his business!

Suzanne, a Sagittarian musician and yoga teacher, pruned deadwood and cleared leaves and debris from the back of her house in her Wealth Gua. She symbolically filled in a missing corner by burying an amethyst crystal in that spot, and placed a decorative stepping stone over it. She patched a large crack on the wall where moisture had been leaking into her closet. And, in her bathroom, she created an altar on the window ledge with purple candles, amethyst crystals and five Chinese coins (five is the wealth number).

As she worked, Suzanne engaged her Sagittarian enthusiasm. "I mindfully and purposefully cleared and prepared the space while holding the strong intention of becoming ready and deserving of wealth." At the moment of the New Moon, she lit the candles and incense, and said a prayer. Shortly thereafter, she was invited to join a new band, and began teaching another weekly yoga class—which added to her income as well as increased her professional confidence and focus.

Minerva, an Aries who runs a goddess center, transformed an unused sauna in her upstairs bathroom into a sumptuous wealth altar. She spread a cloth over the bench, hung a painting of Lakshmi (goddess of wealth), and added a basket of coins, some candles, a chalice of water, an open treasure box, a belly-dance coin belt, and some silk plants. (Note: Silk plants are acceptable; dried plants are not, as they equate to dried-up energy.) She wrote an affirmation for wealth, lit the candles, and spoke her intention, then sealed the energies by burning sage. In the garage below the bathroom she replaced an old, leaky water heater with a new one (leaks in this gua can drain your resources in more ways than one). Since then, she has increased her wealth and tapped into her Aries assertiveness by doing her own seminars.

Leaks in this gua can drain your resources in more ways than one.

Financial flow can increase in a variety of different ways during this cycle. At the New Moon in Taurus, Nadine was preparing for her boyfriend to move in with her, a change which benefits each financially. "I've been clearing my home to make room for him," she said. "At the New Moon I completed the Wealth area and blessed it in anticipation of the coming changes." She lit a green candle and affirmed her desire for financial and relational well-being.

WORKING THE OPPOSITE GUA

On the Bagua map, the Wealth gua is opposite the Helpful People gua. This polarity makes sense when you realize that you can't earn money without the aid of others. We all need helpers to enrich our lives—in this world and the next. At the New Moon in Taurus, it's a good idea to energize your Helpful People gua as well. Write down exactly what you need, including dollar amounts, on a piece of paper, and place it in a silver box in that gua, giving thanks. Or, hang an angel there and ask her to send you more clients.

We all need helpers to enrich our lives—in this world and the next.

SUGGESTED RITUAL FOR THE NEW MOON IN TAURUS:

Grow Your Abundance

You will need: a green or flowering plant, a small piece of amethyst, a hundred dollar bill (or whatever denomination you have access to).

Find a place to sit in your Wealth gua, with the plant beside you. Put the piece of amethyst on top of the bill, take a deep breath, and exhale slowly onto the crystal. Visualize money flowing into your hands.

Then say the following words:

Cash and crystal, on you I blow
My blessings and hopes, a seed to sow.
Bring money to me - let it flow
Like abundant rain, then make it grow.

Give thanks, then bury the crystal in the plant and leave it in your Wealth gua (or put it in the yard outside that gua). Water and care for it well. Put the hundred dollar bill in your wallet, and carry it around for two weeks. Break it at the Full Moon, gratefully affirming your wealth.

WORKSHEET FOR THE NEW MOON IN TAURUS

Gua that is activated for me at this New Moon:

_____

_____

_____

Changes I'll make or enhancements I'll add to this gua and/or its opposite:

1. _____

2. _____

3. _____

4. _____

My intentions for this month related to the New Moon theme:

1. _____

2. _____

3. _____

Results I have manifested:

_____

_____

_____

_____

5 NEW MOON IN GEMINI AND THE KNOWLEDGE GUA

A busy office on Monday morning with phones ringing off the hook. A neighborhood game of "Tag, you're it!" Gemini is a very active sign—both mentally and physically. In Gemini, you're juggling lots of balls and using all your wits to keep them in the air. There are people to call, marketing efforts to make, relatives to visit and local affairs to attend to. After the slow-paced, settled energy of Taurus, you're moving in a faster gear now—and having to attend to the myriad of details that claim your attention.

> **In Gemini, you're juggling lots of balls and using all your wits to keep them in the air.**

At the New Moon in Gemini, it's time to make decisions about everyday matters and engage in discussions to bring about change. A mutable, ever-changing sign, Gemini rules the mental realm—which includes writing, speaking, teaching and local travel. Here we examine the contents of our minds and our belief system. And, we align with the truth and get real with ourselves. Now you'll be getting your immediate environment in order and handling important paperwork. It's also time to tighten or revise your connections with those who matter most to you, especially siblings and other close relatives.

Things to do at the New Moon in Gemini:
- Question the voices in your head
- Start taking or teaching classes
- Get your vision checked
- Buy new office equipment or upgrade your computer
- Send out marketing materials
- Attend networking events
- Get to know your city or local environment

- Join a discussion group on a topic important to you
- Launch a website or blog
- Make a vision board for what you want to create

GEMINI AND THE KNOWLEDGE GUA

Gemini and the third house correlate with the Knowledge gua, located just to the left of your front door. This is the gua you'll be working during this New Moon cycle. Its colors are blue, black and green. Make sure this area is brightly lit, thoroughly dusted (especially your books) and free from clutter, as it represents your mental state and ability to think and communicate.

QUICK FIXES TO ENHANCE THE KNOWLEDGE GUA

- Pictures of your teachers, guides or spiritual mentors
- Books that pertain to what interests you most
- A symbol of a book you'd like to write or skill you'd like to master
- Wood or water elements (related to neighboring guas)
- A meditation pillow or peaceful nook for reading
- Pictures of places you'd like to visit (I associate travel with this gua)
- Your office or a writing desk

Because Gemini rules thinking, now we'll be applying Feng Shui principles to our minds. If you need clarity about something, write down the specifics of what you need at this New Moon (or any other time), and place it in the Knowledge gua in order to stimulate ideas and solutions. This practice is especially helpful with relationship issues, as the Love gua is directly opposite the Knowledge gua, and therefore intimately related (good relationships require good communication). Jot down any dreams, flashes of inspiration or good advice you get in the next few weeks.

An important note: Knowledge is the only area of your house in which single images belong (it's Knowledge and Self-Cultivation, after all). Many people have artwork and photos featuring solitary people or animals scattered throughout their home. If you're single (and would prefer to be happily coupled), these images merely reinforce your status—especially if they're in your Love gua. But in Knowledge, they give you strength. A single image of a spiritual guide, or even of yourself, is appropriate here.

> **Knowledge is the only area of your house in which single images belong.**

During this cycle last year, I took all the books off my bookshelf and dusted each one, which took several hours but completely changed the energy of the room. I also cleaned the shelves and gave away a stack of books. At the New Moon, I wrote down my intentions for a lecture I would be giving, along with new thinking patterns I wanted to establish regarding men. Then, I lit a blue candle and spoke my intentions.

That month was full of intense discussions with both my partner and father, which tested my new thinking patterns to the max. Be careful what you wish for at your New Moon rituals—you may get it! This is especially true at the New Moon in Gemini, when you can make rapid-fire connections between events and witness how your thoughts create your reality. Moving through the challenges with men opened up new lines of communication for us, and my lecture turned out well and led to other speaking opportunities.

INSPIRING RITUALS FROM MY RESEARCH PARTICIPANTS

Several of my research participants reported powerful mental and emotional realizations and clearings at this New Moon.

"I found this exercise very profound," reported Andrea, a Virgo acupuncturist. Her Knowledge gua falls in her bathroom, so she thoroughly cleaned the space and filled it with new plants. For inspiration, she hung a picture of her African teacher on the wall. This powerful shaman symbolizes Andrea's Virgoan healing path, and looking at his image strengthens her educational process.

"The New Moon morning was powerful," Andrea told me. She only had a few minutes to do her ritual, so she lit a candle, burnt sage and said a prayer. "The week after that triggered a deeply rooted issue for me," she noted. "Yesterday the energy was so strong and ready to clear that I danced and prayed (part of my spiritual practice) and most, if not all, of the old issue peeled off."

The New Moon in Eliza's third house was also a solar eclipse on her birthday, which set off shock waves for this Leo. "Just a few days before the eclipse," she related, "I got the news that my job would be ending, so I made a commitment to working fulltime on my business. And, I participated in a group ritual the night before the eclipse, in which I left my fear behind." She blessed her Knowledge gua that night, but didn't move or add anything to it because, she said, it felt 'full' as it was.

"On my birthday," Eliza added, "I got a brilliant idea that I needed to learn how to close the deal to get funding for my project, and a friend gave me the perfect info on how to do this. And, she helped me to overhaul the legal structure of the project. Then, the day after that, I went to see a spiritual teacher who did a "third eye" blessing – putting ash on my forehead – which was very powerful. I feel like the sky is the limit for my new personal year!" Leo is an entrepreneurial fire sign—so working for herself is both appropriate and fulfilling for Eliza.

The New Moon in Gemini is a good cycle in which to gain publicity and attention—one participant was thrilled when a local publication featured him in a major article that month, recognizing the work he had been doing over the years. And, during this cycle another person was asked to teach a series of yoga classes at a new studio, after she'd just completed an advanced teacher training.

Leo is an entrepreneurial fire sign—so working for herself is both appropriate and fulfilling for Eliza.

Robert, an Aquarian, made a vision board which included a picture of the town on the east coast where he wanted to manifest a job. Also, he included the words "alternative health network," since the job he wanted involved the creation of programming for an alternative health TV station. Making a vision board is an appropriate ritual for an airy Aquarius—a sign with stronger thinking and visualizing powers than most. The New Moon activated Robert's office, which he cleared and blessed. Then, he hung the vision board over his desk where he could look at it, and affirm his intentions.

"The day after my ritual," he said, "I called the owner of the TV station, and he said he'd send me a contract in a week! I feel more clarity and peace of mind about the direction my life is taking…this new job is an answer to my prayers for guidance from God."

WORKING THE OPPOSITE GUA

The Knowledge gua is opposite the Love gua on the Bagua map. As previously noted, good communication is essential in a relationship. Therefore, it's a good idea to activate your Love gua as well at the New Moon in Gemini. Add a pair of lovebirds (live or in picture or sculpted form) to symbolize harmonious communion with your mate. Or, if you need a new mate, the New Moon in Gemini is a good time to join an Internet dating site and communicate what you are looking for.

SUGGESTED RITUAL FOR THE NEW MOON IN GEMINI:

Embracing Your Truth

You will need: A blue candle, and a notebook and pen.

Light the candle in your Knowledge gua and thank your spiritual guides for being present (even if you are not aware of them, they do exist!) Take your notebook and write at the top of the page: "Embracing My Truth." Then, ask yourself: Is there anything I'm doing or thinking that is not in alignment with my higher truth? It may relate to your job, marriage, health habits or communication with a friend. Make notes on this for a few minutes. Be honest with yourself. If something isn't working, admit that you just can't do it that way anymore. You don't need to take any action at this time. Just be with the awareness. Then, give thanks to your guides for helping you with this issue and blow out the candle (unless you are letting it burn down).

Listen to your thoughts and feelings throughout the month. If you are angry or frustrated, acknowledge your feelings without forcing yourself to do anything about them. Continue being honest with yourself, and writing in your journal. You may be surprised at the ideas and solutions that occur to you! If you feel guided to do so, make appropriate changes. You are likely to receive further information on your issue at the Full Moon, which tends to bring clarity and culmination.

WORKSHEET FOR THE NEW MOON IN GEMINI

Gua that is activated for me at this New Moon:

_____

_____

_____

Changes I'll make or enhancements I'll add to this gua or its opposite:

1. _____

2. _____

3. _____

4. _____

My intentions for this month related to the New Moon theme:

1. _____

2. _____

3. _____

Results I have manifested:

_____

_____

_____

_____

6 NEW MOON IN CANCER AND THE FAMILY GUA

A cozy bed on a stormy night. The feeling of fulfillment after your favorite meal. Cancer, sign of the Crab (or as I prefer, the curled-up cat!) represents your place of nurturing, where you feel most comfortable, or what feels most familiar to you based on past experiences. It's the foundation of your chart—the ground which stabilizes you. After the hectic, fast-paced energy of Gemini, now you get to slow down and be more introspective.

At the New Moon in Cancer, it's time to take a look at your physical home. Do you feel nurtured there? How can you make it more comfortable? What about your relations with family members? Are there any unresolved childhood issues affecting your current experience?

Cancer is the first of the three water signs. A cardinal, take-charge sign, Cancer is a fierce protector when it comes to family and home—which includes the right to experience peace of mind. During the Cancer cycle, we focus on caring for ourselves and those closest to us. And, we patiently build physical, emotional and financial foundations to support the manifestation of that which we desire.

> During the Cancer cycle, we focus on
> caring for ourselves and those closest to us.

Things to do at the New Moon in Cancer:
- Spring-clean your home, give away old possessions
- Reconnect with friends and activities from your youth
- Spend time "nesting" and rejuvenating at home
- Pursue domestic projects or redecorate your space
- Look for a new residence or property
- Visit and improve relations with family members
- Nurture yourself with healthy meals

- Volunteer for Habitat for Humanity
- Purge yourself of old family patterns and re-parent yourself
- Set up an ancestor altar with pictures of those who have passed on
- Start saving money so you feel more secure

CANCER AND THE FAMILY GUA

Cancer correlates with the Family gua, located in the middle of the left side of your home (from the front door). Its element is wood, and its color is green. Make sure this area is warm and inviting, cozy but not cluttered, and makes you feel at home. Since this gua is associated with having enough money to pay the bills, you don't want any trashy-looking items, unwanted family hand-me-downs or symbols of lack in this area of your home.

QUICK FIXES TO ENHANCE THE FAMILY GUA

- A dining table, perhaps with Grandma's tablecloth on it
- Pictures of family, friends and those who have transitioned
- Family heirlooms (but only if you love them)
- Green plants (but only if they're healthy)
- Images of water, a fountain or fishbowl
- Rectangular or undulating shaped-items
- A well-stocked fridge or cabinets, if your kitchen is here
- Wooden sculptures or furniture
- Items that make you feel emotionally and financially secure

During a previous Cancer New Moon cycle, I focused on healing my relationship with my father. To gain assistance, I turned to my mother, who had passed away three years before. I'd already set up an ancestor altar on my office shelves in the Family gua, with photos and other items related to people I'd loved, now on the other side. I dusted the shelves and polished the pictures, then lit a green candle at the New Moon next to my mother's photo, and asked for her help. I also set out a tiny cup of milk as an offering (an ancient African practice).

Soon relations with Dad reached an all-time low, which astonished me—until I noticed that I'd forgotten to remove the cup of milk, and ants had overrun the altar! Pay attention to the results of your rituals, even if they seem accidental—this development was showing me that I must attend to specifics (ants represent life's details) in my dealings with Dad. As I began to pay closer attention to our joint financial affairs, relations improved and I was able to release certain resentments left over from childhood, giving me a stronger foundation and sense of self.

> **Pay attention to the results of your rituals,
> even if they seem accidental.**

INSPIRING RITUALS FROM MY RESEARCH PARTICIPANTS

Eliza, the Leo we met in the last chapter, focused on healing the past at the New Moon in her fourth house. She lit a green candle and incense and did a meditation at the dining room table in her Family gua. "My intention was to release old, negative family/ancestral patterns while keeping positive, uplifting ones," she explained.

"After the ceremony," she continued, "I had an intense need to throw out things from my childhood—ones I thought I could never release—like yearbooks, pictures, letters, mementos." Eliza also realized how much furniture she still had from the house in which her parents went bankrupt—symbolically hindering her prosperity. She asked her boyfriend to help her get rid of these items, which he was glad to do. "Literally, he's helping me move out old family beliefs and patterns," she observed. This strengthened their relationship, and helped her feel more supported and secure.

> **Eliza realized how much furniture she still had from the house in which her parents went bankrupt—symbolically hindering her prosperity.**

Amy, a Pisces, also bonded more closely with her man after working her Family gua at the New Moon. "I have a wooden bookcase and two rocking chairs in that gua," she told me, "which I painted in various shades of green. Then, my boyfriend's mother came to stay for a few days. By the end of her stay, her true feelings about me were revealed."

Like most Pisces types, Amy has trouble with boundaries. "But I set my limits on how I was to be treated, and things are more out in the open now. I feel truer to myself and have a more solid foundation to work from. And, my boyfriend and I are closer. We understand each other better."

Jim, a Capricorn who likes to build, lives in a yurt next door to his mother's house. His kitchen occupies his Family gua, so he decided to enhance this area by building a stable and attractive storage structure beneath his utility sink.

"The New Moon was the perfect incentive," he said. "I custom built my new sink support a few days prior to it, then at the exact time of the New Moon I made healthy smoothies for my mother and myself and spoke affirmations of gratitude for my family and health. My mother's idiosyncrasies push my buttons on an ongoing basis, but after the ritual I felt a shift in my attitude. A deeper level of compassion toward her came forth."

Denise, a Libra and her husband Sam, a Virgo, spent three weeks doing a complete overhaul of their home during this cycle. "We got rid of non-essential items and cleaned the walls, windows, carpets, drawers, files…everything," she related. "Then, at the New Moon, we lit green candles in our Family gua and blessed the space." That month, Denise met Sam's extended family for the first time, as well as hosting her brother and sister-in-law.

"I have not been involved with my family for years," Denise explained, "so this was a big deal for me." She also had a big blow-out with her son, which upset this Libra's harmony-loving nature. "But we worked through it," she said, "and agreed that our consciousness was raised for better communication. So this month was all about family – and the ritual cemented what was going on."

WORKING THE OPPOSITE GUA

The Creativity and Children gua is opposite the Family gua – children and family go together. If you are having issues with your kids, or with any member of your family, it's a good idea to work this gua at the New Moon as well. Affirm that imaginative ideas are coming your way, and that your creative, childlike spirit is finding just the right solution to your issues. Often just taking time to play with them can improve relations with your children.

SUGGESTED RITUAL FOR THE CANCER NEW MOON

Ancestor Blessing Ritual

You will need: Pictures of one or more ancestors (not necessarily blood relations) to whom you feel a strong connection and whose help you are requesting, a green candle, an offering of food or drink, table settings.

You may wish to cook a special meal for your ancestors (Dad's favorite dish or Mom's signature dessert). Or, keep it simple by pouring Dad's chosen brand of beer or Mom's favorite soda pop. Set places at the table for yourself and the ancestors, preferably in your Family gua. Don't let this ritual spook you; the ancestors want to help us, and are only waiting to be asked. Feeding them is an ancient form of reverence and honor. You may also wish to play music that reminds you of them during the meal.

Light the green candle, and call forth your ancestors by name. Say, "At this New Moon, I honor you and the special place you hold in my heart. I offer you this nourishment and send blessings from this side of the veil." Now, ask them for specific aid. Was Dad a strong, take-charge character? Ask him to give you strength, so you can conquer a challenge you are facing. Was Mom an especially nurturing or insightful person? Request her aid with mending relations between you and a family member.

> **Feeding the ancestors is an ancient form of reverence and honor.**

Serve the food or drink, as if the ancestors were physically present with you. Consume your portion slowly, feeling love and appreciation for your relations. Listen closely for any words of wisdom they might whisper in your ear. When the meal is complete, thank them for their help. You may take their portion of the food to someone who is hungry, leave it outside for animals to consume, or pour the liquids on your plants to nourish them. Blow out the candle, and affirm your problem is solved.

WORKSHEET FOR THE NEW MOON IN CANCER

Gua that is activated for me at this New Moon:

_____

_____

_____

Changes I'll make or enhancements I'll add to this gua or its opposite:

1. _____

2. _____

3. _____

4. _____

My intentions for this month related to the New Moon theme:

1. _____

2. _____

3. _____

Results I have manifested:

_____

_____

_____

_____

7 NEW MOON IN LEO AND THE CREATIVITY AND CHILDREN GUA

Children romping on a sun-drenched playground. A festive celebration with champagne and streamers. Leo represents self-expression and fun. This is where you get creative and come up with original ideas and projects. The child in you comes out, and your relations with young people and romantic relations are emphasized. After the introspective focus of the Cancer cycle, now you're urged to get out and party a little.

At the New Moon in Leo, you're feeling flirtatious and ready for romance. Leo is the second of the three fire signs. A fixed, determined sign, Leo goes after what it desires. Here, we ask for what we want, and open our hearts so we can receive it. My research participants often won at games or received unexpected cash during this cycle. Leo rules gambling and speculation. You roll the dice just because you're feeling lucky—and more often than not, you win!

> **Here, we ask for what we want, and open our hearts so we can receive it.**

Things to do at the New Moon in Leo:
- Visit the local casino or play the lottery
- Ask someone out or plan special dates with your mate
- Begin a creative project such as making a treasure box
- Invest in an entrepreneurial venture
- Host or attend a party or wedding
- Spend more time with your kids—or change the dynamics with them
- Shop for festive, colorful costumes or furnishings
- Put yourself out there as a speaker or creative thinker
- Go dancing or otherwise raise your "fun quotient"
- Attend a festival or take a pleasure trip

LEO AND THE CREATIVITY GUA

Leo correlates with the Creativity and Children gua, located in the middle of the right side of your home (from the front door). This is the gua you'll be working during this New Moon cycle. Its element is metal, and its color is white. Make sure this area is bright, clean, uncluttered and inviting. It should be a playful space in which you can be creative, that brings out your sense of joy in life and makes others feel inspired as well.

QUICK FIXES TO ENHANCE THE CREATIVITY GUA

- Original artwork by yourself, your kids or others
- Metal fixtures, furniture or instruments
- A metal bell — to ring when you need creative inspiration
- White or yellow flowers in a metal vase
- Pictures of baby animals or children
- Round or square objects
- Yellow and earthy elements
- Games, crafts and sports equipment
- A stereo or computer to play your favorite music
- Books on creativity, children or becoming more youthful
- Pet beds, jungle gyms or stuffed animals

At my former residence, the Creativity gua fell in my bathroom. Prior to the New Moon, I added a playful shower curtain featuring images of leaping dolphins, and hung a piece of art I'd made on the wall. At the moment of the New Moon, I lit a white candle, took a bubble bath and gave thanks for more fun and romance in my life.

I attended two wedding celebrations during that New Moon cycle, making it especially festive. And, my man and I renewed our romantic feelings by spending more time together being playful—watching movies, playing Scrabble, going boating. Also, in an interesting twist, I did several astrology readings that month in which I helped clients improve relations with their children.

INSPIRING RITUALS FROM MY RESEARCH PARTICIPANTS

Tracy is a practical Capricorn. Her Creativity and Children gua falls in her living room, which features a large bookcase where she performed her ritual. "Since the fifth house is romance, gambling and creativity," she said, "I lit a love candle and put my Lotto dream board and pot o' gold on the shelf, then hung a heart with two flowers on the wall."

Tracey reported good news on the money front. "No other way to explain this random event. Yesterday, I got a call from a former employer saying that they were dismantling their retirement program and that they fully vested me and would be sending me about $6600. That was unexpected! Since I'd already received a disbursement from them, I thought my vesting was done."

Tracey's ritual produced financial, rather than romantic, results—despite the fact that Leo is associated with romance. Though my participants' Leo New Moon rituals brought more fun and life to existing romances, none of these rituals reeled in new lovers. Yet several people experienced financial windfalls or gambling wins.

Francine, a Sagittarian, was one who lucked out on the money front. Her Creativity gua lies in her bathroom, which is decorated in an Egyptian theme. "It's already filled with round, square, earth and white elements," she noted. "I just traded the red roses in the vase for white ones and took the pointy-headed cockatoo off the wall. As I was considering the 'speculation' aspect of this gua, I took a closer look at the shower curtains and suddenly realized the design is made up of money plants!"

At the New Moon, Francine lit a white candle and

invoked greater prosperity. Because her speculative Sagittarian Sun is located near abundant Venus in her natal chart (not to mention the presence of money plants in her Creativity gua), Francine is often lucky at gambling. A few days after her ritual, she went to a local casino and won $2500. The next day she went back and won $1000. Then, a week later, she unexpectedly received a check for property taxes she had overpaid. The ritual enhanced her inherent luck.

> **A few days after her ritual, Francine went to a local casino and won $2500.**

Tina, a level-headed Capricorn with a theatrical Leo Moon, got creative at this New Moon, which activated the area of her home containing her closet. "I purged, cleaned and reorganized it the day before," she said. "Then, when the New Moon was exact the next evening, I stepped into my closet behind the gold fabric curtain that is my door. As if coming out on stage, I flung back the curtain, stepped out and sang the words, "In the garden of my dreams, many sweet things blossom. In the garden of my dreams, life unfolds—it's awesome!"

The next morning, Tina received a powerful insight about a particular chapter in a book she was writing. Also, she was suddenly inspired to paint her outdoor shower (just outside the Creativity gua) in 'cosmic berry,' a shade of purple. "I had a blast doing it and it looks spectacular!" she said.

Curtis, a determined Scorpio, is a writer and astrologer new to his town; he needed to become known. At the New Moon in Leo, he set up an altar in his Creativity corner with a microphone, quill pen, astrology dice and his business card. Soon after his ritual, each symbol bore fruit. An article he'd written was accepted by a local magazine (the quill pen), he received an invitation to speak (the microphone) at an event, and got several new clients (the astrology dice). "I've been aiming at these things for some time," he said. "The article and lecture are non-paying opportunities, but I'm confident they'll bring success."

Other participants focused on their children at this New Moon—one took a pleasure trip with her husband in the hope of getting pregnant (results still pending!), another performed a ritual to release her attachment to her 17-year-old son, who was soon to leave home, and yet another went on a camping trip with his teenaged sons and bonded more closely with them.

WORKING THE OPPOSITE GUA

As noted in the previous chapter, the Creativity and Children gua is opposite the Family gua. Especially if you are dealing with an issue regarding a child, work the Family gua at this New Moon as well. Place a photo of your child in Family and write down what you are affirming. Ask the ancestors to bring about improvements that fulfill the highest good of all concerned.

> **Especially if you are dealing with an issue regarding a child, work the Family gua at this New Moon as well.**

SUGGESTED RITUAL FOR THE NEW MOON IN LEO

Balloon Bliss

You will need: A small bottle of bergamot or sandalwood oil. Five brightly colored flat balloons to blow up (or, you can use helium-filled balloons). Paper for writing down your intentions, rubber bands and fun, upbeat music.

The sign of Leo is all about creating more joy in our lives. This ritual is intended to reawaken your childlike wonder and sense of fun, which will lend power to your intentions.

At the New Moon, after you have cleaned and prepared your Creativity gua, sit down in that area and list five qualities you want more of, each on a small piece of paper. For example, perhaps you'd like more laughter, tolerance, joy, inspiration and abundance. When you are finished writing, choose a different color balloon to represent each quality you seek. Then, blow up each balloon, magnifying each quality as you blow. Tie each wish onto a balloon. Then, anoint it with the essential oil you have chosen. Arrange the balloons in your Creativity gua however you like, either tied together as a festive bunch, or hanging from strings throughout the gua.

Dance until joy is suffused throughout your being.

Next, put on your favorite, upbeat music and dance your wishes into your body. Laugh, shout, jump around and really feel these qualities take root in your being. Inhale the blissful scent of the essential oil. Dance until joy is suffused throughout your being. Then, give thanks for the fulfillment of your wishes. You can leave the balloons up for as long as you like, but be sure to remove them when they start to go limp.

WORKSHEET FOR THE NEW MOON IN LEO

Gua that is activated for me at this New Moon:

_____

_____

_____

Changes I'll make or enhancements I'll add to this gua or its opposite:

1. _____

2. _____

3. _____

4. _____

My intentions for this month related to the New Moon theme:

1. _____

2. _____

3. _____

Results I have manifested:

_____

_____

_____

_____

8 NEW MOON IN VIRGO AND THE HEALTH GUA

A volunteer picking up litter from the side of the road. An avid gardener weeding her plot of land. The sixth house is the place of well-being and satisfying service. It's where you get health and work in order by examining and changing fundamental habit patterns. The Virgo New Moon inspires you toward order, health and fitness—and gives you the energy to accomplish these goals. After the fun, playful vibe of Leo, now you buckle down and get to work, while learning to take better care of yourself.

At the New Moon in Virgo, it's time to make a difference in your own life and the lives of others. Virgo is the second of the three earth signs. This mutable, flexible sign asks what it can do to help (though we have to take care to not help too much!) In the Virgo cycle, we donate our time to a good cause, or work overtime to accomplish tasks and projects. My clients and research participants made progress on health and employment goals during this cycle. When you work it, Virgo works for you!

> At the New Moon in Virgo, it's time to make a difference in your own life and the lives of others.

Things to do at the New Moon in Virgo:
- Embark on a health campaign or body cleanse
- Take a fitness boot camp or do regular yoga
- See a new health practitioner or do healing practices
- Make your work space more tidy and efficient
- Volunteer with a local non-profit or charity
- Apply for jobs and go on interviews
- Begin work-related training
- Take more responsibility for pets or people in your care

- Thoroughly dust and clean your home and office
- Weed and prune your garden
- Get plenty of rest and treat yourself better

VIRGO AND THE HEALTH GUA

Virgo correlates with the Health gua, located in the center of your home. This is the central, life-giving axis around which the other eight guas spin. Its element is earth, and its colors are yellow and earth tones. As it is associated with both health and work, this area must be kept clear and immaculate. Check carefully for hidden sources of grime or dust (heaters, carpet, overhead fans, storage areas) in this gua, to boost your well-being.

> **As it is associated with both health and work, this area must be kept clear and immaculate.**

QUICK FIXES TO ENHANCE THE HEALTH GUA

- A potted plant with yellow flowers
- A picture that invokes health, perhaps a beautiful scene
- A bowl of lemons, oranges or other healthy fruit
- Workout equipment
- A salt lamp, left on at all times
- Vitamins or an herb garden
- Ceramic pots and sculptures
- Square, triangular and horizontal objects
- Bright, fiery themes (perhaps red or orange candles)

At the last New Moon in Virgo, I removed the coffee pot from my Health gua, as I wanted to eliminate caffeine from my diet. And, I added an Astro Feng Shui treasure box I'd made to strengthen this aspect of my astrological work. Also, I removed the heater grate and cleaned away the dust and cobwebs that had accumulated inside. I lit a yellow candle and placed it on the kitchen counter along with my written intentions for health and work, then burned sage to bless the area.

Since that time, I've had renewed inspiration for this book. As mentioned elsewhere, adding a fresh green plant to my Knowledge sector also helped. And, I hired a new health practitioner to help me heal some chronic physical issues (which required giving up coffee, of course!)

Change often comes slowly. Don't despair if you haven't reached your goal by the end of this New Moon cycle, or any other. Congratulate yourself for small wins after you do your monthly rituals, and remember that you'll have more opportunities to work each gua as time goes on.

> **Don't despair if you haven't reached your goal by the end of this New Moon cycle, or any other. Congratulate yourself for small wins.**

INSPIRING RITUALS FROM MY RESEARCH PARTICIPANTS

In astrology, work and health are intimately connected—they both relate to habit patterns and how we spend our energies. Rituals can be performed for either or both of those areas of life at the New Moon in Virgo.

Vera, a pioneering Aries with communicative Gemini rising, wrote an affirmation for her "perfect job" at this New Moon, put the paper under the rug in the middle of her home—and with typical Aries speed, found a job the next day! Communication planet Mercury was retrograde at the time, though, so she had to await the results of fingerprinting and a background check before beginning the new position.

Be patient when performing New Moon rituals during the thrice-yearly Mercury retrograde periods, as results may take longer to manifest. (This is especially true for those with Gemini and Virgo Sun or Ascendant, since they are ruled by "winged messenger" Mercury.) The retrograde periods of this planet through 2020 are listed at the back of this book.

Be patient when performing New Moon rituals during the thrice-yearly Mercury retrograde periods, as results may take longer to manifest.

Nadine, a luxury-loving Libra, had just returned from a trip to Turkey with a beautiful new tablecloth. At the New Moon in Virgo, she draped the cloth on her coffee table at the center of her home, sat at her altar and invoked increased financial prosperity. Though Virgo is not considered a money sign, it does rule work and service—and this cycle brought Nadine an unexpected offer to manage a small yoga studio, improving her financial picture.

Martin, a Scorpio realtor, lit an orange 7-day candle at this New Moon, and left it to burn on a table in the center of his home. "The image says 'Our Lady of Real Estate,' he chuckled. "It was given to me by a former client, and has an image of a corporate-type realtor holding a set of keys and contracts, with a halo over her head and a big dollar sign over the halo. It seemed the perfect symbol for the ritual."

Scorpios are usually good at creating money for others. And, the fact that the candle was given to Martin by a former client was an added plus, symbolically. After his ritual, said Martin, "I can't believe how much my work has picked up during this cycle, despite the housing crisis! This stuff really works!"

Scorpios are usually good at creating money for others.

Louise, an imaginative Leo, worked the health angle at

the New Moon in Virgo—and also received an unexpected work opportunity. She performed her ritual at a bookshelf in the center of her home. To add the metal element related to this gua, she lit yellow candles on an old iron cook stove. Then, she invoked healthier eating habits and weight loss. "This process has made me aware of and receptive to subtle shifts in energy," she reported. "I am making wiser choices in terms of eating and drinking. And, I even have a promising job interview scheduled next week."

Margie, an earthy Taurus, set up an altar in her Health gua at the New Moon in Virgo. She added a vase of daisies and plumeria from her garden (many Taureans love to garden), a statue of Kuan Yin (the goddess of healing and mercy), a bowl of lemons and a note listing her New Moon intentions. They included: Negative results for a malignancy on her upcoming CT scan, and the discovery of an early (treatable) cancer for her friend Martha, who had already been diagnosed with the disease.

Delighted, Margie reported that both intentions got positive results! Note: When setting intentions for others, be sure the other person is in alignment with what you are intending. That was true in this case. "This altar was a daily reminder of my intentions and prayers, and a great comfort," said Margie. It was fun to get phone calls about the results throughout the two weeks before the Full Moon!"

> **When setting intentions for others, be sure the other person is in alignment with what you are intending.**

Olivia's Health gua falls in the entryway to the home she shares with her husband, Ross. A Capricorn massage therapist with several spiritually-oriented Aquarius planets in her chart, at the New Moon Olivia put earth-toned candles in the empty candle holder in the entryway, and to bless the space, hung a beautiful picture of Jesus coming out of a lotus flower. Then, she and Ross drove to Mt. Shasta to celebrate their anniversary.

"In Shasta," Olivia related, "I had an amazing awakening experience with an esoteric teacher. Once we returned, I felt inspired to create a new business dedicated to Awakening. After putting it off for years, I finally felt clear and began creating a web site."

WORKING THE OPPOSITE GUA

The Health gua has no opposite point. Because its borders touch all the guas, however, you can also work whichever gua is calling out for healing during this cycle. For example, if there is a need for better health either emotionally or physically within your family, work your Family gua in addition to your Health gua at the New Moon.

SUGGESTED RITUAL FOR THE NEW MOON IN VIRGO

Focused Relaxation

You will need: Sage leaves or packaged sage tea, a yellow candle, lavender essential oil, relaxing music.

First, make sure your Health gua has been thoroughly cleansed and prepared. Then, boil water, pour it over the tea and let it steep while you do the relaxation exercise. Place the cup in your Health gua, and light the yellow candle. Then, put on your relaxing music and position yourself comfortably in a prone position on a couch, bed or the floor. Anoint your upper lip with lavender oil so you can inhale its relaxing qualities.

Give yourself about ten minutes for this simple but amazingly powerful process. Take a few deep breaths, then direct your attention to your feet. Hold your focus there briefly while you feel your feet relax. Then, as you move upward, do the same for each body part, in this order: Ankles, calves, thighs, pelvis and belly, lower back, middle back, upper back and chest, back of the neck, back of the head, top of the head, forehead, eyes and behind the eyes, nose, mouth and jaw, tongue, throat and behind the throat, tops of the shoulders, upper arms, lower arms, hands. Continue breathing deeply and slowly throughout this exercise.

When you have finished, rise slowly and take your cup of tea. Sit in or near the Health gua, and think about your New Moon intentions for greater health, relaxation or work fulfillment as you sip your tea. Gaze at the candle as you meditate on the improvements you wish to make. You may also write your intentions down, and place them near the candle. Repeat the focused relaxation process any time you feel stressed. Doing this practice for even five minutes can make a big difference for your health and well being.

WORKSHEET FOR THE NEW MOON IN VIRGO

Gua that is activated for me at this New Moon:

_____

_____

_____

Changes I'll make or enhancements I'll add to this gua or its opposite:

1. _____

2. _____

3. _____

4. _____

My intentions for this month related to the New Moon theme:

1. _____

2. _____

3. _____

Results I have manifested:

_____

_____

_____

9 NEW MOON IN LIBRA AND THE LOVE GUA

A happy couple enjoying a romantic picnic under a tree. Two business partners signing a win-win contract. In Libra, we join forces with another person, for better or worse. Here we find balance—by seeing ourselves reflected in others. Libra tests your ability to give and take, and also reveals your shadow—disowned parts of yourself. After the work and health-oriented focus of Virgo, in Libra we learn to share and become more loving.

> **In Libra, we join forces with another person, for better or worse.**

At the New Moon in Libra, you feel the desire to merge with another. Libra is second of the three air signs. A cardinal, peace-loving sign, Libra seeks to create more balance through communication. Here, we work through our relationship differences and learn to balance each others' strengths and weaknesses. My research participants made significant relationship shifts during this cycle—from attracting new partners to deepening existing ties and, when necessary, even ending relationships.

Things to do at the New Moon in Libra:
- Get engaged or married
- Join a dating site and meet new people
- Make a list of your priorities in a partner
- Have a heart-to-heart talk with your mate
- Make a treasure map featuring happy couples
- Release old reminders of past relationships
- Look closely at what others are reflecting back to you
- Engage in friendly conversations with people you meet
- Plan intimate encounters with your mate
- Read Calling in the One (see Recommended

Resources)
- Seek an agent, lawyer or representative
- Investigate forming a new business partnership
- Complete a relationship so you can move on

NEW MOON IN LIBRA AND THE LOVE GUA

Libra correlates with the Love gua, located in the furthest right hand corner from the front door of your home. This gua symbolizes your relationships—even if it falls in the garage or bathroom! Its colors are romantic shades of pink, burgundy, lilac and peach. It's time to add romance to this gua, even if it's only a red ribbon tied around the sink pipes, a pink nightlight in the bathroom, or a rose-colored heart hung in the corner of the garage.

> **This gua symbolizes your relationships—
> even if it falls in the garage or bathroom!**

QUICK FIXES TO ENHANCE THE LOVE GUA

- Things in pairs—candles, animal statues, end tables
- Festive items—shiny ribbons, dancing shoes, a bottle of Champagne
- A framed picture of you and your beloved in a sexy pose
- A pink faceted crystal hanging in the far right corner of the room
- Fresh flowers with a compelling scent
- A bowl of Hershey's kisses
- Pink or red wall hangings or bedding
- Pictures of romantic scenes or couples, perhaps in a treasure map
- If there is a TV in this room, cover it with a pretty scarf

At the last New Moon in Libra, I broke up with my partner. I removed items from my Love gua associated with him—a back massager he'd given me and a book we'd enjoyed reading together. I also moved the patio love seat, where we often cuddled, out of the Love gua and into Helpful People. As the New Moon approached, I carefully cleaned all the items in my Love gua—sconces filled with silk flowers, matching end tables and a picture of Gustav Klimt's "The Kiss"—and replaced the stubby pink candles with new ones. I stripped the bed and washed the bedding, and bought new pillows (this releases your former partner's energy, and clears the space).

At the moment of the New Moon, I lit the new candles and invoked the loving release of my partner and the healing of our hearts. The Love gua is, first and foremost, about the deep and abiding love for oneself. This ritual helped me forgive both my partner and myself, and begin to move on.

> **The Love gua is, first and foremost, about the deep and abiding love for oneself.**

INSPIRING RITUALS FROM MY RESEARCH PARTICIPANTS

Olivia and Ross, who appeared in the last chapter, moved in together not long after they met. A year later, Olivia, a tradition-loving Capricorn, longed for marriage—but Ross, a Taurus who liked to take his time, still wasn't ready. The romance had lost its pizzazz. The couple's bedroom fell in the Love gua—a perfect location. But, the power spot (furthest right hand corner of the room) held nothing that symbolized a loving relationship.

Just prior to the New Moon in Libra, I encouraged Olivia to remove the abstract painting and green lamp in that corner, and exchange them for romantic items and images in shades of pink or red.

The power spot (furthest right hand corner of the room) held nothing that symbolized a loving relationship.

A month later, I received an excited call. "We're engaged!" Olivia announced. She had enlarged and framed a photo of herself and Ross in a sexy pose, and hung it on the wall. And, she replaced the green lamp with a pink one and hung a rose-colored curtain behind the bed. "The bedroom feels so different," she confided, "and our love life has really picked up. But it was still a shock when he gave me the ring!"

Maggie, a long-suffering Pisces whose two older children still lived with her when we met, hadn't been in a relationship for years. She'd set up a home office in her bedroom, her Love gua. To get to the bed, she had to navigate an obstacle course of file cabinets and computer equipment. She even had to climb over a treadmill to reach the bathroom!

Maggie didn't seem to have much room in her life for love, but she surprised me. At the New Moon, she sectioned off the home office with a curtain, and relocated some of the equipment. Then, she hung a romantic painting of lovers over her bed, added two pink candles and rose quartz crystals to the headboard shelves—and began folding up the tread-mill when not in use. Soon she had me do a love match comparison with a man she'd met on a dating site—and choose an auspicious wedding date! They are now happily married, and Maggie's kids are on their own.

Maggie didn't seem to have much room in her life for love, but she surprised me.

Grace, the Virgo writer, placed colorful pinwheels outside her Love gua (which falls in a storeroom) and affirmed that the wind would blow her a new kind of love. She washed away cobwebs and put shocking pink paper on the window sill—and suddenly the room glowed pink! She added a pair of dolphins, pink carnations and candles, which she lit at the New Moon.

A week later Grace's long-time golf partner, dying of emphysema, sent her $5000. Visiting him in the hospital, she tenderly stroked his face. "We'd never been that close," she related. "A surge of love filled me; I felt high for days. This is the new perspective on love I'd prayed for!"

Louise and Jake's ceremony led to the awareness that their 20-year marriage had run its course. The New Moon was a solar eclipse on her birthday—a double whammy with life-changing impact. "I made the altar in the corner of our bedroom," said Louise, a creative Leo, "using pairs of things and a pink scarf. We had been going through a semi-remote period for months, so doing a small ritual was a nice way to reconnect. We lit the candles, and decided we'd like to find a better balance in our relationship."

Results came swiftly. "Even though our marriage had been going through changes," said Louise, "I never expected it would end." The couple decided that she would move to their property in Northern California to give them both time to reflect. "It's a good thing," Louise related, "at least for me, but the idea of divorce is scary. I'm not sure where it's all leading."

The New Moon in Libra marked a turning point for Francine, a Sagittarian. Since her husband's death years ago, she had been living, surrounded by his belongings, in the home they'd shared. Her Love gua was a shrine to Civil War memorabilia—including several antique guns! You definitely don't want this energy here. The guns didn't bother Francine, yet visitors were unsettled by them. She admitted that her love life had long been stale—yet she was content on her own, without a partner.

> **Her Love gua was a shrine to Civil War memorabilia—including several antique guns!**

Still, at the New Moon in Libra, Francine resolved to make some changes. She gathered up all the family photos in the Love gua and boxed them up, and took down several dark, depressing pictures. Then she hung up a pretty pair of floral prints, put a Sinatra CD in the jukebox, and began playing love songs every day. "They take me back to romantic adventures I had in the 60s and 70s," she explained. The guns were next to go, she assured me.

For her New Moon ceremony, Francine lit candles and incense, and affirmed that loving vibes were coming to her. A week later, she went to a high school reunion and had a great time with old friends. And, she reported that she has begun to love herself more. "I've decided I'm going to reinvent myself. And, I've been making more time to see friends." She also stopped seeing folks who brought her down. Plus, the "gambling hunch" struck again, and she won $4700 at a local casino. "Everything turns to money for me," she laughed. "I'm not even going to try and figure out why."

Working her Love gua produced sexy results for Eliza, the budding Leo businesswoman. "My relationship with my boyfriend was going well," she said, "but I thought it would be fun to spice up my Love gua and see what happened. Previously, this gua was pretty, but more on the spiritual side. So I added a picture of a couple in a Tantric pose, plus some erotic books and purple candles."

At the New Moon, Eliza lit some "desire" incense, and got instant results. "My boyfriend called to say we should have sex more often. And since then, things have been really hot and heavy!"

WORKING THE OPPOSITE GUA

As previously noted, the Knowledge gua is opposite the Love gua. If you've been experiencing any communication issues with your partner, work this gua too. Add green plants, burn a blue candle and affirm your intentions.

SUGGESTED RITUAL FOR THE NEW MOON IN LIBRA

Feeling the Love

You will need: a yard of pretty pink fabric and a yard of pink ribbon, five small pieces of rose quartz, a bottle of rose essential oil and a pink candle.

As an astrologer, I often hear from desperate folks who long for a lasting romance, when the real problem lies within—with a lack of self-love that prevents them from attracting a loving partner. As astrologer Caroline Casey says in her brilliant book, Making the Gods Work for You, "Love unites us with the community, whereas romance addiction isolates us; we seek total fulfillment through another and, consumed in small dramas, neglect to give our gift to the community."

With this in mind, I am not going to give you a traditional love spell for this New Moon. Instead, the following ritual will open your heart and strengthen your love for yourself and others.

Cut the pink fabric into five pieces, about 5" by 5". Then, cut the ribbon into five, 5" pieces. Light the pink candle in your Love gua, and anoint it with rose oil. In addition, anoint the stones with rose oil, as you think loving thoughts. Place each stone into the center of a square of fabric, and tie it with a piece of ribbon. Put one bag on your altar in the Love gua, affirming love for yourself. Blow out the candle or let it burn down.

Give the other four bags to people you love, telling them how you feel. Include your mate, if you have one. If not, give three of the bags to people you love, and put the fourth in the Love gua along with your bag. Give thanks to Venus, the goddess of love, for sending you all the love you need. You may feel inspired to do loving things for your community over the next few weeks. Take advantage of the chance to generate good karma.

WORKSHEET FOR THE NEW MOON IN LIBRA

Gua that is activated for me at this New Moon:

_____

_____

_____

Changes I'll make or enhancements I'll add to this gua or its opposite:

1. _____

2. _____

3. _____

4. _____

My intentions for this month related to the New Moon theme:

1. _____

2. _____

3. _____

Results I have manifested:

_____

_____

_____

_____

10 NEW MOON IN SCORPIO AND THE WEALTH GUA

A miner digging for gold in the depths of a cave. An exhausted midwife facilitating a long, drawn-out birth.

Scorpio is deep and mysterious. This sign symbolizes that which is hidden from view, as well as the right use of power. It rules the continuum of birth, death and rebirth. Here, we become enriched—either by making money, sharing resources or exploring the psyche. But, something must usually be sacrificed for something new to be born. In Scorpio, we make deeper commitments to ourselves and others. We learn how to share power. After the more mental and conceptual focus of Libra, now we lay it on the line emotionally and financially.

> **With Scorpio, we become enriched—**
> **either by making money, sharing resources**
> **or exploring the psyche.**

At the New Moon in Scorpio, you feel inner rumblings, a call for change. Scorpio is the second of three water signs. A fixed, determined sign, Scorpio gets to the bottom of things by bulldozing whatever stands in the way of progress. Here, we plumb our psyches for truth and purge our lives of the superficial or extraneous. My research participants made powerful, often scary shifts during this cycle. Facing the Scorpio void isn't easy, yet results in a tremendous payoff.

Things to do at the New Moon in Scorpio:
- Make major purchases or investments
- Bury the past and birth something new
- Commit emotionally or financially to a partnership
- Give away old possessions
- Get hypnosis or some other in-depth therapy
- Release or transform a relationship
- Take up martial arts or run a marathon

- Have sex and/or get pregnant
- Volunteer with hospice
- Transform your life, perhaps by relocating

SCORPIO AND THE WEALTH GUA

At this New Moon, you'll be working your Wealth gua (located in the furthest left hand corner from the front door of your home). This gua symbolizes prosperity and well being—and therefore must be carefully maintained. Its colors are purple, red, green and gold. Because Scorpio and Taurus are both associated with the Wealth gua, you can enhance this gua with the same Quick Fixes I offered in Chapter Four.

I moved to a new home at the last New Moon in Scorpio—a marathon effort that pushed me to my limits, physically and emotionally. Though I was too busy to perform a ritual that month, I did let go of old possessions, and purchased new ones. For the first ten days of the cycle, my car was in the shop. I was driving a loaner vehicle—which amplified my feeling of being on unsteady ground. Nothing was familiar. Yet friends and family stopped by with housewarming gifts (prosperity comes in many forms!) and several new clients called for consultations.

By the time my car came home at the Full Moon, freshly detailed and looking like new, I'd settled into my new place and was feeling stronger—ready for a new phase of life.

INSPIRING RITUALS FROM MY
RESEARCH PARTICIPANTS

Sheila, a freedom-loving Sagittarian, was finally able to let go of an unfulfilling relationship during her Scorpio New Moon cycle—and as the emotional burden lifted, her design business became more prosperous. Sheila's Wealth gua falls in her bathroom. At the New Moon, she cleaned that gua thoroughly and burned sage for purification, then tied red ribbons around the pipes under the sink and plugged the sink and bathtub with drain stoppers (to symbolically keep her wealth ch'i from leaking out). She hung rich new purple towels she'd bought for the occasion, lit a purple candle and invoked wealth and happiness.

Even though she didn't ask for a break-up, the ritual helped Sheila let go of her partner. "I was hanging on to a man who cannot commit and cannot communicate. After the ritual, I felt I could move on from him—and doing so unblocked the dam to my prosperity. Suddenly, I have more work than I know what to do with!" Sagittarian types often attract people who can't commit, due to their own loss-of-freedom fears. To avoid repeating the same scenario, Sheila needs to choose her partners wisely in the future.

> **"After the ritual, I felt I could move on from him—and doing so unblocked the dam to my prosperity."**

On the morning of the New Moon in Scorpio, Ellen's husband Tim sat down on the bed to put on his socks, when the old bed suddenly collapsed! The couple was dismayed at the thought of purchasing a new one, as finances had been tight. In rapid succession, a water heater also needed replacing and both of their vehicles required expensive repairs. Luckily, they had enough cash to cover these unexpected expenses, but weren't able to save any money.

"All of these expenses were the result of long-term decay and/or neglect," observed Ellen, an astrologer. "I think of Scorpio as reflecting an investment of time and resources," she added. "The cracking of the bed set off a chain of events that led to a much-needed investment in the infrastructure of our lives. I've noticed that every time we've used Feng Shui, the initial results are a disaster – nasty stuff is stirred up, like lancing a boil. Then the dust settles, and things improve."

"The cracking of the bed set off a chain of events that led to a much-needed investment in the infrastructure of our lives."

Barbara, a Gemini editor, helped boost her partner's wealth at the New Moon in Scorpio. She placed a vase of purple lilacs on a table in her Wealth gua before dashing off to work, and said a quick prayer for prosperity. "My husband has a business making highly sophisticated telescopes and equipment for amateur astronomers," she told me. "His sales depend on individuals' discretionary income and are anything but recession-proof. Within a few days, however, he got some serious inquiries and a new order!" Gemini, sign of the Twins, may have better luck than other signs at manifesting results for significant others.

Just prior to this New Moon, George, a Taurus, discovered that he had to spend several thousand dollars to remove a tree encroaching on his neighbor's property. Recalling his Wealth gua was about to be activated, he simply affirmed that he'd win the money.

"I just got back from a four-day trip to Reno," he related, "and I won close to $4000!"

Before leaving on his trip, George had created an altar in his laundry room (Wealth gua) with a treasure chest full of coins, then lit a green candle at the New Moon and affirmed that his financial needs were met. Not only did he win at the casinos, but during that cycle, George also received several unexpected checks in the mail.

After doing their rituals, several other participants won money or received unexpected checks. One received $10,000 from two different sources, and another won a $17,000 jackpot. Just before she won, this woman's husband had taken a photo of her with a handful of cash, and placed it on their newly created Wealth altar with other prosperity symbols.

> **Not only did he win at the casinos, but during that cycle, George also received several unexpected checks in the mail.**

The next story illustrates how Scorpio connects to both death and money. Soon after her father's passing, Lana, an intuitive Pisces, did a meditation, tuning in to him. She now knows where her father is. "He's in the electrical wires of all the rural co-ops across the U.S. He spent his career building those co-ops. I've been at odds with what happens at death. Now I have peace, as I know his spirit is everywhere."

At the New Moon, to honor her dad, Lana placed flowers in her bathroom (which corresponds to her Wealth gua). The following day, her mother called. "Lo and behold," said Lana in amazement, "I'm getting $500 a month from my father's annuity! It may be small, but it's also very helpful."

WORKING THE OPPOSITE GUA

As noted in Chapter Four, the Wealth gua is opposite the Helpful People gua. If you need help banishing unwanted circumstances or manifesting greater prosperity, hang an angel in this gua and ask for her aid. Or, write down what you need and place the paper in your silver box, asking for help.

SUGGESTED RITUAL FOR THE SCORPIO NEW MOON

Bury the Past

You will need: A shovel or spade and a place to dig. An item that symbolizes what you're releasing, a piece of paper on which you have written your intentions, and matches or a lighter. Do this ritual at night, either in your backyard or a public place like a park or even a graveyard, which nicely fits the Scorpio theme of death and rebirth.

Scorpio demands a sacrifice before bestowing its blessings. Therefore, at this New Moon you will be letting go of something or someone to which you are attached—or even addicted. This could be a lover who isn't good for you, a food or drink you can't live without, or an old attitude about money that's standing in the way of your wealth.

> **Scorpio demands a sacrifice before bestowing its blessings.**

Decide what you are ready to sacrifice, and imagine how you'll feel once you're free of it. When you're clear, write down what you are releasing, and what blessings you'd like to trade for your freedom (Scorpio loves to barter). Find an item that represents what you are releasing (such as a bag of potato chips, or a picture of your former flame). Dig a hole a few feet deep and sit next to it, with your item and paper in hand. Call on Pluto, the ruler of Scorpio, to aid your quest. Tell Pluto your sorrows, your difficulties with this attachment or addiction, and how much you need relief. Pour your feelings down the hole. Shedding tears will fertilize the rite.

Now read what's on your paper, set it on fire and throw it in the hole. Once the paper has burned down, say goodbye to your symbolic item, add it to the grave, then fill in the hole. Give thanks to Mother Earth for composting your offering. And, thank Pluto for giving you the strength to let go of the past and transform your life.

WORKSHEET FOR THE NEW MOON IN SCORPIO

Gua that is activated for me at this New Moon:

_____

_____

_____

Changes I'll make or enhancements I'll add to this gua or its opposite:

1. _____

2. _____

3. _____

4. _____

My intentions for this month related to the New Moon theme:

1. _____

2. _____

3. _____

Results I have manifested:

_____

_____

_____

_____

11 NEW MOON IN SAGITTARIUS AND THE KNOWLEDGE GUA

A perceptive Indian scout surveying the path ahead. A fiery teacher delivering an awe-inspiring lecture. Representing the higher mind, Sagittarius broadens our horizons. This sign emphasizes teaching and learning, international travel and publishing. Here, we are stimulated by new ideas, intuitive insights and cultural differences. We aim high during this cycle—and sometimes overshoot our target. But inevitably, we learn and grow. Now it's time to deliver your message to whoever will listen. After the more intense and emotional Scorpio cycle, we break free and breathe easier in Sagittarius, finding our freedom.

At this New Moon, we embrace new faces and places. Sagittarius is the last of the three fire signs. A mutable, restless sign, Sagittarius longs for the open road and seeks out challenges. Now is the time to sign up for classes, take trips and explore new spiritual paths. My research participants broke out of old ruts and belief systems during this cycle—and made progress toward being seen and heard.

> **We aim high during this cycle—and sometimes overshoot our target. But inevitably, we learn and grow.**

Things to do at the New Moon in Sagittarius:
- Plan or take a long-distance journey
- Read an inspiring biography or historical romance
- Sign up for classes or further training
- Give talks and seminars, perhaps on radio or TV
- Spend time in nature or ride horses
- Make a "bucket list" of things to accomplish before you die
- Create a website or otherwise promote yourself
- Listen to subliminal CDs to release old belief systems

- Join a writer's group or book club
- Further your knowledge about legal matters or languages
- Create a vision board

SAGITTARIUS AND THE KNOWLEDGE GUA

At the New Moon in Sagittarius, you'll work the Knowledge gua, just to the left of your front door area. This gua symbolizes wisdom and intuitive knowing. Its colors are blue, green and black. Here we focus on tapping in to our higher minds, as well as teaching and traveling. (Travel is usually associated with the Helpful People gua—but it made more sense to me to link it with the Knowledge gua and the sign of Sagittarius.) You may use the same Quick Fixes for this gua as offered in Chapter Five, since both Gemini and Sagittarius are associated with the Knowledge gua.

At a recent Sagittarius New Moon, I hung a beautiful, nature-themed wall hanging in my Knowledge gua. Then, I wrote out my intentions for a class I'd be giving that month at a bookstore, lit a blue candle and sent my request for success to the Universe. I also sent a query letter to a magazine about an article I wanted to write.

I began practicing EFT (Emotional Freedom Technique), which helped me ferret out and release old beliefs. The class I energized at the New Moon was cancelled due to lack of sign-ups; I realized the venue wasn't right for me and refocused my energies. Don't despair if specific things you invoke for don't pan out. This usually means you are being led to something more suited for you. That month, I was asked to give an impromptu talk that was well received and brought me several new clients. And, the magazine I queried responded with a request for the proposed article, which was later published with a link to my web site, enhancing my client base.

INSPIRING RITUALS FROM MY RESEARCH PARTICIPANTS

"My ceremony began with making a list of things I want to know," said Annette, an Aries writer. "Most of what I wrote was about knowing a world I've only imagined. Then I listed things I want to say, and how that would help bring about the world I imagine. This list included traveling to different countries. I then burned the lists, sending my thoughts into the Universe." She also added a rock shaped like a mountain to her Knowledge gua, which reminded her of a life-changing trip she'd taken.

> **We think of Aries as being bold by nature—
> but this is not always true. In Annette's case,
> the call to adventure had to be cultivated.**

The results, said Annette, were subtle yet effective. "I'm getting some coaching on allowing myself to be seen in the world – a huge part of manifesting my dream of connecting with people globally. I'm having a great time playing with 'being seen,' and the book I'm writing is almost complete." We think of Aries as being bold by nature—but this is not always true. In Annette's case, the call to adventure had to be cultivated.

At the appropriate New Moon, Adam, a clever Gemini, devised an innovative way of letting go of old, limiting belief systems. "I've been listening to subliminal CDs, and releasing old thoughts and perceptions," he said. "For the ritual, I put three trash cans in my Knowledge gua, which falls in my garage – one blue, one black and one green. Then, I intended that I am 'trashing' old beliefs—and I am seeing a difference!"

Last year at the Sagittarius New Moon, Olivia, the Capricorn massage therapist profiled earlier, set her intention to step out as a spiritual teacher. "I put some books on my altar next to a statue of Kuan Yin, and began reading one on channeling that I've pushed aside for years. I've almost finished a new website, focusing on bodywork and somatic counseling. Things are flowing in a very easy to understand and advanced manner, reflecting the depth of what I do. The website is a huge success—and new clients are calling me!"

Lilly's Knowledge gua falls in her kitchen. While she was away on a long-distance trip during this New Moon cycle, she had that part of her home remodeled. An instinctive Pisces, Lilly didn't realize she was working the appropriate gua—or even that she was traveling during the appropriate cycle. I find that people often enact their cycles without consciously knowing it. The combination of fresh vistas and her lovely, more spacious kitchen cleared Lilly's mind—triggering new ideas for a business project.

> **I find that people often enact their cycles without consciously knowing it.**

Other participants furthered their careers by learning new things during this cycle—Sagittarius represents where we open out to the world. One person lit a blue candle in her office at the New Moon and immediately was asked to give several talks; she also committed herself to having marketing photos taken. At the Sagittarius New Moon, another learned how to burn CDs on her laptop—a skill which will come in handy for her work. Someone else attended an out-of-town screenwriter's convention, where he became part of a group of writers who invited him to join their group. And, he's making progress on a screenplay that he'd long been trying to write.

WORKING THE OPPOSITE GUA

As noted in Chapter Five, the Knowledge gua is opposite the Love gua. If your relationship could benefit from improved communication or you are seeking a new partner, work the Love gua as well as the Knowledge gua at the New Moon.

SUGGESTED RITUAL FOR THE SAGITTARIUS NEW MOON

Make a Treasure Map

You will need: magazines, a poster board of any size, glue stick, scissors, glitter glue (the ones for fabrics work best) or other decorations. If you're going to frame your creation, choose the appropriate-sized frame and board.

Treasure-mapping is a perfect activity for a Sagittarius New Moon, which is about looking at the big picture of your life. Also called a vision board, a treasure map magnetizes new possibilities into being. You can make one for something specific—such as a new home, relationship or job—or simply for something you want more of, such as peace, love or health.

First, decide which goal to focus on. Then, peruse magazines for corresponding images and words. Rather than letting your logical mind prevail, allow the unconscious mind to participate. Breathe deep, let go and ask the Archer for guidance. Even if an image doesn't seem to relate to the theme, yet it speaks to you strongly, tear it out. Choose more images than you will ultimately include. Once you have a pile of images and words, begin arranging them on the board in ways that feel right. Then, paste them down with glue stick. If desired, add affirmations with a felt-tipped pen.

> **Rather than letting your logical mind prevail, allow the unconscious mind to participate.**

When you're complete, you can outline images with glitter glue or paste down other items. Then, post your creation someplace you'll look at it daily, like the refrigerator or over your desk. Your subconscious mind will attract what you've pictured; be patient, though, as the process can take time.

WORKSHEET FOR THE NEW MOON IN SAGITTARIUS

Gua that is activated for me at this New Moon:

_____

_____

_____

Changes I'll make or enhancements I'll add to this gua or its opposite:

1. _____

2. _____

3. _____

4. _____

My intentions for this month related to the New Moon theme:

1. _____

2. _____

3. _____

Results I have manifested:

_____

_____

_____

_____

12 NEW MOON IN CAPRICORN AND THE FAME GUA

A respected businesswoman receiving a civic award. A proud father at a family gathering. Capricorn represents career status and recognition for one's efforts. This is where we shine—with our business, reputation and calling in life. We reap the results of the hard work we've done, while continuing the climb to success. Now it's time to survey our attainments and reassess our direction. In the Capricorn cycle, it's good to toot your own horn—and bask in the praise you receive. After the free-wheeling and spirited Sagittarius cycle, we buckle down, working to achieve our goals.

At the New Moon in Capricorn, go after what you really want in life. Capricorn is the last of the three earth signs. A cardinal, determined sign, it is practical and grounded. Now we take concrete steps to advance our career and reputation. During this cycle, my research participants became serious about their purpose in life, and many received acknowledgment affirming they were on the right path.

> Now it's time to survey our attainments
> and reassess our direction.

Things to do at the New Moon in Capricorn:
- Decide what's most important to you and pursue it
- Revamp your workspace and get organized
- Create an updated resume, listing your accomplishments
- Print professional business fliers or marketing materials
- Make peace with your father or other authority figures
- Take on responsibility for a business or community project
- Work hard toward achieving a goal

- Purchase items to enhance your career
- Build something solid or reinforce foundations
- Contact publications about featuring your work
- Frame certificates you've earned to hang in your Fame gua

CAPRICORN AND THE FAME GUA

At this New Moon in Capricorn, you'll be working your Fame gua, located directly opposite your Career gua or front door (or the middle of the house on which the front door is located). The Fame gua symbolizes recognition for your efforts. Its element is fire, and its color is red. Here, we're called to stand out, be courageous and pursue our highest goals.

QUICK FIXES TO ENHANCE THE FAME GUA

- Symbols of your highest calling or chosen career
- Fire elements, like a heater, BBQ or incense burner
- Red candles, drapery or furniture
- Pointed things, like cacti, swords or pictures of mountains
- Wooden or green elements
- Animals skins or pictures, to enhance your courage
- Pictures of accomplished people who you admire
- A red envelope containing your written intentions

At a recent New Moon in Capricorn, I found a fabulous, Bagua-shaped mirror at Cost Plus and hung it in my Fame gua. Some say mirrors are not good in this gua, as they symbolize water (water douses fire), but this mirror felt intuitively right for me. I knew it would magnify my intentions. Trust your intuition over any rules you read in a book, including this one.

Trust your intuition over any rules you read in a book, including this one.

At the New Moon, I lit a red candle and affirmed the success of two business projects I was working on. A few days later, I was interviewed for the San Diego Astrological Society's newsletter. Then, I received word that The Mountain Astrologer would be publishing my Astro Feng Shui article in an upcoming issue. My monthly website essay was especially well received, and 12 new clients contacted me for consultations! I was in demand during the entire cycle. (Note: The mirror served its purpose well in Fame; I later moved it to my Health gua and assigned it a different task—to repel the stressful noise of my neighbors—a job which it performed equally well.)

INSPIRING RITUALS FROM MY RESEARCH PARTICIPANTS

During the Fame cycle, we often confront our feelings about being known for our work or losing our privacy—as Janice, a Leo artist, discovered.

"Redecorating my Fame gua was a difficult process," she confided. The area directly opposite Janice's front door features a fireplace—which is appropriate, since fire is the element associated with this gua. "I decided to repaint the drywall around the fireplace using a red Venetian plaster," she said. "The product was harder to work with than I had anticipated. I had to do many layers and it took several days rather than the few hours I had allotted. I'm still not sure I'm happy with it. Then I decorated the mantle with my art and candles, and did a New Moon ritual concentrating on my goals for my art career."

Though Leo is an outgoing sign, self-confidence can be elusive and may need development.

Soon, Janice received a commission for a painting, and was asked to exhibit her work in two shows. A road trip to visit art galleries proved challenging, however. "It was really up and down," she said. "I didn't realize the inner conflicts I have about fame! I became aware of the emotional roller-coaster ride I experience on a regular basis." Though Leo is an outgoing sign, self-confidence can be elusive and may need development.

Other signs can experience self-doubt in the Fame cycle, as well. Though Grace, our Virgo writer, had been doing her craft for 40 years, she never felt sure of herself—perhaps, she surmised, due to difficult relations with her father that had affected her confidence in her writing talent.

For her ritual, she said, "The first thing I did was sprinkle salt in both the Career and Fame areas and offer prayers of forgiveness for Dad and me." "Then I brought in huge bouquets of evergreen boughs—the scent was heavenly! Next, I enlarged my desk space, covered it with red metallic paper, created an 'important to-do basket', set up a new computer that had been in its box since I bought it months ago, and posted flyers of my writing workshops and mock-ups of two forthcoming books on the wall above my computer."

Her hard work was rewarded. At the Full Moon, Grace received a letter from a foundation to which she'd submitted a grant proposal months prior, notifying her that she would soon receive a check for $6000 to complete one of her book projects!

Sometimes during this cycle, events will propel us toward our higher calling. Ken, a Pisces writer who specializes in gemology, was working at a rock shop when, at the Capricorn New Moon, he got laid off. "Within a few days, though," he reported, "I was offered a scholarship from the International School of Gemology. The president felt I'm 'doing important work' and wants to work with me in the future. That was a biggie! Getting laid off was a blessing, as everything in my life is pointing toward my need to keep writing."

Alana, an Aries spiritual teacher, got clear on her calling in life during this New Moon cycle. "In the Fame area," she said, "I put up my red and green OM plaque. Then I set up an altar on a round wooden table with statues of Kuan Yin, Spider Woman and Isis. I added a 7-day candle and did a ceremony to draw in what the Divine Feminine wanted me to do in my path of service and career."

During the Fame cycle, what Alana called her New Moon "altarations" helped her clarify her purpose: To express her pioneering Aries nature by creating a world-wide forum for wise women, so they can share their formerly secret and sacred prophecies and wisdom. All of Alana's activities now dovetail with this higher purpose.

Be particularly attentive to what lives in your Fame gua. One person was storing her adult son's belongings in a closet in this gua—and spending much of her time trying to help him get situated in life. The closet was also full of clothes from a former career; needless to say, she was having a hard time moving forward. Releasing the clothes as well as her son's belongings gave this woman new momentum. A couple had an attached garage in their Fame gua, containing junky trash cans. They moved the trash cans to an outdoor shed and bought a new hose. Both of their efforts became more focused during this cycle, as their energy stopped leaking out—which boosted their careers and reputations.

> Be particularly attentive to what lives in
> your Fame gua.

WORKING THE OPPOSITE GUA

Since Fame is directly opposite Career on the Bagua map, these two guas are intimately connected. The intentions we activate at the New Moon in Aries are often fulfilled during our Capricorn Fame cycle. Borrow a bit of Fame's fire now, and tie a red ribbon to your front door knob or porch light (or something else in your Career gua), to strengthen both ends of this spectrum.

SUGGESTED RITUAL FOR THE NEW MOON IN CAPRICORN

Tooting Your Horn

You will need: Access to a computer, or pen and paper, and a red candle.

As we have seen, being recognized for your accomplishments, talents or opinions can bring up insecurities. This New Moon is about courage and putting yourself out there. We'll start on a small scale to avoid triggering any unmanageable fears. This ritual will prepare you to tackle even bigger goals in the future. You have several options. Choose the one that feels most appropriate for you:

- Write a letter to the editor of your local paper about a timely issue that matters to you. Be bolder than usual in the way you express yourself.
- Do a blog or Facebook post, expressing a potentially controversial opinion about something, or tooting your own horn in some way.
- Approach an authority figure about hiring you, or buying, publicizing or representing your work. Express confidence in your abilities.

At the New Moon, light a red candle and affirm your courageous next step, along with the results you'd like to see in terms of acknowledgement and recognition. Then, follow through, do what's required to manifest your intentions, and see what happens!

WORKSHEET FOR THE NEW MOON IN CAPRICORN

Gua that is activated for me at this New Moon:

_____

_____

_____

Changes I'll make or enhancements I'll add to this gua or its opposite:

1. _____

2. _____

3. _____

4. _____

My intentions for this month related to the New Moon theme:

1. _____

2. _____

3. _____

Results I have manifested:

_____

_____

_____

_____

13 NEW MOON IN AQUARIUS AND THE HELPFUL PEOPLE GUA

A group of friends pitching in, helping with a move. A fundraising dinner to launch an after-school program for kids. In the Aquarius cycle, we pull together with others to make dreams come true, as we focus on community efforts, friendships and ideals. Here, we ask for help—and give it in return. We enlist others' aid to attain our goals. And, we take stock of our dreams and decide which ones are worth pursuing. After the serious, work-oriented Capricorn cycle, we explore our social selves, have fun with friends and like-minded others—as well as giving something back to the community.

> **Here, we ask for help—and give it in return.**

At the New Moon in Aquarius, you envision a better future for yourself and the world. Aquarius is the last of the three air signs (despite its symbol, the Water-bearer, Aquarius is an air sign). A fixed, intellectual sign, Aquarius makes connections between seemingly disparate elements and people. During this cycle, my research participants learned to ask for the help they needed, and involved themselves in productive group events.

Things to do at the New Moon in Aquarius:
- Host or attend a community event
- Go after a long-held dream
- Unite with others to pursue a common cause
- Call on friends, allies and guides to help you out
- Join a networking website or support group
- Be a Helpful Person to others
- Buy a computer, add Facebook friends or join Twitter
- Make a silver treasure box to hold your intentions

- Get back in touch with old friends
- Offer to barter services with others

AQUARIUS AND THE HELPFUL PEOPLE GUA

At the New Moon in Aquarius, you'll be working your Helpful People gua, located to the right of your front door as you enter. This gua symbolizes friends, community, dreams and help from the beyond. Its colors are silver, gray and white. At this New Moon we ask for magic, and often receive it!

QUICK FIXES TO ENHANCE THE HELPFUL PEOPLE GUA

- Angel figures or other helpful beings
- Beautiful or useful things friends have given you
- A silver box or container for your intentions
- A bell, signifying that your requests will be heard
- Gray or silver lamps or furniture
- Silver stones, like mica or hematite
- A collage with pictures of your friends or helpers
- Business cards – yours and others'
- Business or client files
- Symbols of projects you're dreaming of, or could use help with

At the most recent New Moon in Aquarius, I wrote down two goals on a piece of paper and placed it in the silver treasure box in my Helpful People gua. Then, I invoked aid (especially from my angelic Mama on the other side) in fulfilling my hopes. One was short term: to get my neighbor to stop playing his electric guitar while I was trying to relax in the evenings. The other was long term: to further my big dream of building an earthen, sustainable home and community.

Personal requests to my neighbor had fallen on deaf ears

(perhaps literally!) so I enlisted my helpful landlord during this cycle to address the noise problem. After that, the noise lessened a bit. Just when I was resigned to accept my fate, I received word that my neighbor would be moving soon. Also, that month I planned a trip to southern New Mexico to scout locations for a possible move. Details smoothly fell into place as I coordinated my schedule with that of my travel buddy.

INSPIRING RITUALS FROM MY RESEARCH PARTICIPANTS

At the New Moon in Aquarius, Katie, an adventurous Sagittarian, added some silvery curtains and angel figurines to her Helpful People gua. She reported that people went out of their way to help her that month. Katie had recently broken her foot while mountain-climbing. "I made a connection with a friend's podiatrist," she said. "He looked at my foot for free and even gave me a free boot, saving me about $600. This is incredible, as I don't have health insurance! Also, outside sources helped me write my business plan, design my label and write the text for my website."

Linda, a Virgo massage therapist, cleared trash and clutter from her patio at the Aquarius New Moon. She also buried a crystal outside her Helpful People gua to symbolically fill in the missing corner. "While sitting in that area, I lit a white candle and stated my intentions: To attract and recognize all people, angels and helpers that are presented to me and to act on any appropriate ideas they bring or inspire in me. Also, to attract clients, both new and former, and to further others' healing path as well as my own."

During that moon cycle, Linda said, "I have trusted the incredible guidance I received and acted accordingly. I felt very supported. I made some great connections with new clients, many old clients have called to book sessions, and my schedule has been full."

Marie, a Cancerian realtor, added touches of silver and white to her living room in her Helpful People gua, and hung an angel for help from the other side. Then, at the New Moon, she spontaneously added file folders pertaining to difficult clients.

"I'd been feeling so beaten down, so I told the Universe, 'I need help!'" Marie told me. Soon, to her astonishment, she heard from each client. "The inactive ones paid me for my time and left, like magic," she reported. "Then, at the Full Moon, two of four pending offers were accepted, and are now in escrow!"

Lydia, the Aries psychologist, attended a conference in Zurich at this New Moon. Before she left, she lit a candle in her Helpful People gua and affirmed success for her trip. "I am still on fire with all the helpful people and potential projects that are in the works," she enthused. "This conference was the first time I've been on a collaborative panel, and the other participants praised me for wrapping up the panel with an awesome speech. I was invited to the 'in-group' farewell party and met the top people in my field. There is even talk of my going to the World Congress next year. This is the next career level that I've been praying for!"

Alana, the spiritual teacher we met earlier, set up an altar on a shelf in her guest bathroom at the Aquarius New Moon. "I added a white and silver angel, a photograph of my grandparents, 'star' candle holders with white candles in them, and a silver 'love' box with my intentions," she said.

> **"I feel more centered and focused, knowing that support from other realms is available."**

Soon after, she reported, "I had an uplifting experience at my Moon Lodge, and we did a great job raising funds at the health fair to assist our teacher. I've been having vivid and full dreams, and I feel more centered and focused, knowing that support from other realms is available. The exercise helped me acknowledge that support and ask for guidance."

Greta, another Cancerian, enhanced her Helpful People gua with a mirror and a white lace cloth upon which she placed two angels, a white shell, quartz crystals and a silver, heart-shaped box. She wrote down her big dreams, read them aloud at the New Moon and placed the list inside the box.

That month, Greta said, "I increased my Internet presence and talked up my business and dream projects. I doubled my number of friends on Facebook, opened a Twitter account, increased the number of hits to my web site, and made some important contacts that are vital to reaching my goals. I didn't reach every goal I set, but overall, I'm very pleased."

WORKING THE OPPOSITE GUA

The Wealth gua is opposite the Helpful People gua, so to invoke more prosperity at this New Moon, you may wish add an enhancement to your Wealth gua, like a chunk of amethyst or healthy green plant. Be specific in what you need, including the amount, and you're more likely to get results.

SUGGESTED RITUAL FOR THE AQUARIUS NEW MOON

Calling The Angels

You will need: a white or silver pillar candle, a silver box, an angel figure or picture, a paper on which you've written your needs, and harp or other ethereal music.

We're entering the angelic realm at this New Moon, where we ask for help in making our wildest dreams come true, or in handling our most pressing mundane concerns. Purify yourself before this ritual by bathing in scented salts or oil, then dress in flowing white or pastel garments.

Sit in your Helpful People gua (which you have already cleansed and de-cluttered), put on the music and light the candle. Ask the angelic realm to be present at your ritual. You can call on particular guides like Archangel Michael or Gabriel, or an ancestor who serves as a guardian angel for you. Gaze at your angelic image as you tune in to that realm. Then, read your list, asking for the specific aid you require. This may be something like, "Please protect me in my upcoming journey," or "Please bring me $1200 by the end of this month." You can also ask for help for other people.

When you're complete, put the paper into the silver box, and blow out the candle. Thank the angels for the fulfillment of your wishes.

WORKSHEET FOR THE NEW MOON IN AQUARIUS

Gua that is activated for me at this New Moon:

_____

_____

_____

Changes I'll make or enhancements I'll add to this gua or its opposite:

1. _____

2. _____

3. _____

4. _____

My intentions for this month related to the New Moon theme:

1. _____

2. _____

3. _____

Results I have manifested:

_____

_____

_____

_____

14 NEW MOON IN PISCES AND THE HEALTH GUA

A dolphin gliding beneath the surface of a wave. A woman deep in prayer at a meditation garden. With Pisces, we step back from the world and tap into our deepest selves. The last sign of the zodiac, Pisces rules completion, spiritual health and behind-the-scenes activities. Here, we tune into our internal guidance system as well as other dimensions of reality. After the social whirl of the Aquarius cycle, we allow ourselves to coast a bit—to turn within and regroup. Rather than force things to happen, we rest and rejuvenate. However, we must take care not to let our fears run away with us during this cycle. There's mystery in the air now—the trick is to relax and surrender to it.

At the New Moon in Pisces, we sense life's deeper meaning. Pisces is the last of the three water signs. A mutable, emotional sign, Pisces has compassion for those less fortunate, and wants to help and heal others. Here, we also explore our artistic and musical sides and pay attention to our dreams. During this cycle, my research participants found more meaning in life, healed their body/minds and lifted their spirits.

> There's mystery in the air now—the trick
> is to relax and surrender to it.

Things to do at the New Moon in Pisces:
- Take a relaxing vacation – preferably near water
- Do a cleansing fast or purification
- Write down and analyze your nightly dreams
- Get healing treatments and massages
- Allow yourself to sleep more
- Turn off electronic devices and enjoy the silence
- Open your heart to those less fortunate
- Forgive others as an act of healing for yourself
- Make preparations, do research or soul-searching

- Get inspired—go dancing, do art projects or make music

PISCES AND THE HEALTH GUA

Just as you did at the New Moon in Virgo, you'll be working your Health gua, the center of your home. Pisces is associated with spiritual and mental health, but also extends to physical well being. The Health gua's element is earth and its colors are yellow and earth tones. Use the same Quick Fixes for this gua as offered in Chapter Eight.

At a recent New Moon in Pisces, I scrutinized my kitchen counter in the center of my home. Although I'd already Feng Shui'd it, I knew something had to be amiss as I'd been sick twice in the past few months. Then it hit me: The lung infection began after I'd hung a new picture in that gua, of a hill in Africa where "nipples" had been added to two large mounds resembling breasts. I'd thought it was a positive feminine symbol, but now I realized it had subconsciously made me feel exposed. Feng Shui can be quite literal—if a particular part of your body is ailing, check your Health gua for clues! After trading the picture for another featuring Diana's healing temple at Ephesus, I've had no further lung problems.

> **Feng Shui can be quite literal—if a particular part of your body is ailing, check your Health gua for clues!**

At the New Moon, I lit a yellow candle and affirmed health. During that cycle, I was inspired to do a physical cleanse. During a week-long retreat at a friend's house, I soaked in the spa, did yoga daily and worked on a writing project in a leisurely fashion.

INSPIRING RITUALS FROM MY RESEARCH PARTICIPANTS

As Lydia, the Aries therapist, was preparing for her twelfth house ritual, she was surprised to find a client sitting in her living room. "I'd forgotten I'd scheduled him! He had just received the news that he needed spinal surgery; his spirits were low. I spent the hour in what felt like a spiritual reading, channeling information on how to prepare for and heal from the surgery. He was smiling when he left—a bright light encircled him."

Later, Lydia lamented to a friend that she hadn't been able to do her ritual. Her friend replied, "That was your ritual! You were doing your true work." Lydia told me, "I knew that to be true. Since then, I've felt physically stronger, more aligned with Source."

A Pisces ritual can bring surprises or reveal hidden truths. Katie, the adventurous Sagittarian, also had an unexpected experience. "On the morning of the New Moon," she told me, "I was violently ill. I realized that I was purging the leftover poison from past experiences and beliefs. As I was metaphysically shifting gears, so was my body. As soon as I was able to crawl out of bed, I lit a white candle placed in the center of my home. I experienced no other illness that month. I also regained mobility with my foot as it completed its healing."

> **A Pisces ritual can bring surprises or reveal hidden truths.**

At this New Moon, Robert, an Aquarian, covered a wooden table at the center of his home with a brick red cloth and placed two orange candles on it. He wrote down affirmations about his physical and spiritual health, then while burning sage in his Health gua, he spoke them aloud.

"During this cycle," he reported, "I stopped taking the anti-depressants I'd been on for 12 years." (He had slowly been reducing the dosage). "I had a few mood swings after that, but they quickly passed. Now, my spiritual and physical health are in good shape. I'm really impressed by this result!"

Tish, the Virgo expressive arts therapist, found a tie-in between her physical and financial health. At the New Moon in Pisces, she worked its spiritual angle. "I hung religious medallions that belonged to my parents at the center of my home, my dining room. At the New Moon, I lit a saint's candle there and said a prayer for healing."

Since then, she reports, "I have implemented a change in how I view my business. Now I'm focusing on love and connection rather than money. And that has been very helpful. It gets me out of my fears around money and more into my spirit—and my finances are growing!"

> **"Now I'm focusing on love and connection rather than money."**

Pisces also represents a culmination of one's past efforts, as Marie discovered. "My work day ran much longer than planned," she said, "and I was in my car at the moment of the New Moon. So I shot an intention heavenward for spiritual health."

A Libra, Marie is focused on seeking balance. That week, she felt prompted to call her "spiritual cleansing lady" for an appointment, to get back to feeling strong and centered. "Also," she related, "my job showed signs of dissolving and a future career direction emerged—a culmination of the last three New Moons. I didn't do a formal ritual this time, but things seem to have happened anyway." The Pisces cycle often brings things to completion, as we rest and integrate what we have received.

Greta, the sensitive Cancerian we met in the last chapter, worked her Health gua at the Pisces New Moon. "I discovered that the exact center of my home is my telephone, which hangs on the wall in my kitchen," she said. "I think this is significant, since communication is such an important part of my life and health." (Greta works as a HelpLine attorney). She cleaned the area and smudged it with sage, then added a jade plant in a yellow ceramic planter and placed quartz crystals on top of a piece of harvest-colored fabric.

The Pisces cycle often brings things to completion, as we rest and integrate what we have received.

"At the New Moon," said Greta, who practices yoga, "I lit a candle and stood in the area in Mountain Pose for eleven minutes and envisioned perfect health pulsing through my body."

The results of this ritual were perplexing at first. The following night at a belly dance class, Greta's left hip began to hurt, and the pain continued through the next week. And, a severe rash broke out on her left leg. A doctor visit revealed that she had shingles, caused by the awakening of a dormant virus from childhood chicken pox. While she was recuperating, Greta did some intense soul-searching to dissolve and heal the pain from her past.

"Though it started out rocky," she told me, "this cycle has ended with a complete recovery from the shingles, a five pound weight loss, and now, after releasing the past, every cell in my body is singing, dancing and smiling!"

Once again, don't despair if your ritual produces strange results at first. As Greta discovered, health flare-ups create opportunities to heal and improve our well being. And, Pisces introspection is the key to this healing.

Health flare-ups create opportunities to heal and improve our well being.

WORKING THE OPPOSITE GUA

The Health gua has no opposite point. Because its borders touch all the guas, however, you can also work whichever gua needs healing during this cycle. For example, if you're longing to have a better social life and seeking new friends, work the Helpful People gua as well as the Health gua at the New Moon.

SUGGESTED RITUAL FOR THE PISCES NEW MOON

Water Gazing

You will need: A dark glass or ceramic bowl, water from a spring, lake or other natural source, a fresh-cut twig, yellow candle, nature-themed music and your favorite incense.

Water gazing, or scrying, is an ancient divination technique for accessing the depths of the subconscious mind or getting messages from the beyond. This ritual should be done at night. People used to scry on the surface of a lake by moonlight. In this ritual, we'll be scrying indoors using water from a natural source. Ideally, this should be rainwater, well water or water from a lake or stream, but bottled spring water also works.

At the New Moon, light your yellow candle in your Health gua, and find a comfortable spot to sit and scry for a half hour or so. Light your favorite incense, and put on music that reminds you of nature. Place the candle near your scrying bowl to illuminate your task. All other lights should be kept low or off.

Formulate a question about something that's been troubling you—your health or another topic. Take a few deep breaths to center yourself, then stir the water with your twig. Once it becomes smooth again, stare at the water's surface. Soft-focusing your eyes may help you "see." Continue staring, holding your question in mind, until you see an image or a shape that speaks to you, or you receive a strong feeling impression. Let your intuition interpret this message. Be patient, to see if another message wants to appear. When you feel complete, blow out the candle and give thanks for the inspiration you've received, however subtle or mysterious. Watch your dreams for further revelations about what your message might mean.

WORKSHEET FOR THE NEW MOON IN PISCES

Gua that is activated for me at this New Moon:

_____

_____

_____

Changes I'll make or enhancements I'll add to this gua or its opposite:

1. _____

2. _____

3. _____

4. _____

My intentions for this month related to the New Moon theme:

1. _____

2. _____

3. _____

Results I have manifested:

_____

_____

_____

_____

A FINAL WORD

Congratulations! You have completed a full cycle of Astro Feng Shui. Now, you get to start all over again! As the wheel turns, you'll have more opportunities to tweak and energize different parts of your life and home. Now it's time to look back on your wins—big and small—and assess what still needs to be done.

MY BIGGEST WINS FROM THE LAST 12 MONTHS:

_____

_____

_____

_____

SMALL WINS THAT INDICATE PROGRESS:

_____

_____

_____

_____

GOALS I'D STILL LIKE TO MANIFEST:

_____

_____

_____

_____

ASTRO FENG SHUI Q & A

Dear Simone,

I've been using your Astro Feng Shui system for two years with great results; however my home is a continual mess and my career sucks. While on a house-sitting job, I realized that I come into a beautiful home and make a mess, with stuff spilled, dumped, on floor, on counters, tables – everywhere in the house.

Can you offer me some wisdom on how to enhance both my home and my career? I'm sick and tired of living in a dumpster.

Grace

Dear Grace,

Thank you for being so faithful to the AFS system! In your natal chart, the ruler of your Family gua or fourth house (which shows the kind of home you would have) is very near chaotic Uranus in the ninth house (Knowledge gua). No wonder there's always chaos in your home! Therefore, the issue begins in your mind. Make sure your Knowledge gua is as tranquil, beautiful and serene as possible - and keep it that way. This must be a no-clutter zone, the place you go to meditate and relax each day. Hang a picture, perhaps from nature, that calms your mind. Write down your intentions for a clear, serene home and a successful career. Then, channel that boisterous Uranus energy into your work - don't be afraid to go out on the edge. Be daring in your writing, to feed your muse so it doesn't have to wreak so much havoc in your environment.

Good luck!
Simone

Dear Simone,

This may be a problem everybody wishes they had, but it's frustrating to do Astro Feng Shui rituals in different areas of my house, while the only results I produce consistently are financial ones. Even if I do a ritual in another gua, it shows up as money. Is it possible to get stuck, and not be able to move to another area of life, or is this a temporary situation? (I'm not complaining about the money, I'd like for that to continue, but there must be some way of lighting up another area in my life.) Incidentally, I started having luck with gambling about ten years ago.

Sue

Dear Sue,

You are blessed with a Sun/Venus conjunction in Sagittarius in the ninth house (Knowledge gua), with Venus ruling your eighth house (Wealth gua) of other peoples' money. A trine from Jupiter in your fifth house of gambling to Mars in your eighth house adds to your inherent luck. This propensity got triggered ten years ago when your progressed Sun entered Aquarius to harmonize with your natal Sun/Venus. Because money has come so easily to you since then, you've grown accustomed to receiving your blessings in this way.

To expand your way of receiving, you must change your beliefs. Luckily, the upcoming Sagittarius New Moon activates your Knowledge gua, so now's the time to affirm something new. Write down an affirmation like, "I give thanks for expanded blessings in the form of renewed health" (or whatever you need) and place it in this gua. Add a statue of Ganesh, the Hindu elephant god, to help overcome obstacles. During the week before the New Moon, light a white candle each day to Ganesh, repeat your affirmation and give thanks for his help. At the New Moon, leave an offering of sweet fruit or yogurt for him, and eat the blessed food the next day. You may need to repeat the affirmation for a while, until the new belief takes root in your subconscious mind. Don't worry that you'll lose your financial blessings – they should continue for at least the next 20 years!

Good luck!
Simone

Dear Simone,

In general, I am feeling really good lately and work is going well. But I do have one problem: my two car garage is a huge, dirty mess. It is filled with building supplies as my husband uses it to store his unused materials and stuff that's heading to the dump or charity. Therefore we cannot fit our cars in the garage and we park them outside in the driveway, making it impossible to keep them clean. Also, this week I ran over a nail and woke up to discover a flat tire!

The garage is in the left half of the front of the house. The house is shaped like a box, so the garage takes up half of the front. There is a planter box and entry on the right half. The front door needs repair and cleaning and the planters have overgrown and dead plants!! And, relations with my husband haven't been great these days, as he has been frustrated with his work. What do you recommend?

Lisa

Dear Lisa,

It's amazing that you are doing so well, given the state of the front of your house! You've got messy building materials in your Knowledge gua, keeping you from thinking clearly and/or blocking communication with your mate, and a semi-functional front door with dead or overgrown plants in your

Helpful People gua! And, both situations spill over into your Career gua as well. If only for your husband's sake and the well being of your marriage, it's time to get to work!

The next two New Moons will trigger your Knowledge gua and Fame gua. Since Knowledge is connected to Love, and Fame is connected to Career, this is a good time to address your situation. Begin with the front door, the all-important "mouth of ch'i." Have it repaired and cleaned. Remove the dead plants and trim back the overgrown ones or add healthy, new ones. Get a Helpful Person to aid you in this process.

Then, have a heart-to-heart talk with your husband. Explain how the state of the garage is distressing you and leaving the cars exposed to the elements – without blaming him. Enlist his help in figuring out a solution, perhaps a storage shed. At least get him to take away the charity donations. If he is uncooperative, just bless the garage at the next New Moon, set an intention for what you want, burn some sage and give thanks for resolution. He will likely come around if he doesn't feel pressured. You may be surprised by how things improve for both of you, if you keep affirming what you need and let things unfold.

Good luck!
Simone

p.s. Lisa reported that before she even mentioned the issue, her husband began cleaning out the garage! And, after clearing the dead plants from her Career gua, she received a call approving her admission to the prestigious "Relocation Team" at her real estate office.

Dear Simone,

My condo used to be pretty and neat. But for the last 9 years (since 2001), it's been going downhill. In the last three years especially, my piles of paper/mail have gotten worse and worse. Now it's approaching serious clutter.

I seem completely unable to attack this situation, get rid of the clutter, and deal with the incoming mail on a daily basis.

Can you shed any light on this devolution?

Shelly

Dear Shelly,

Nine years ago your progressed Sun, in late degrees of mysterious Scorpio, entered your 12th house – a deep, watery place associated with the past and the unconscious mind. It sounds like your clutter problem is a reflection of some old or deeply buried issues you don't want to face. Once your progressed Sun enters Sagittarius at the first of next year, these issues are apt to become quite clear—and you'll probably feel that you're able to take action.

With Pisces so strong at the root of your chart, you easily feel overwhelmed at home. You do not lack for Virgo planets (the neat-and-tidy gene), but they're all in your tenth house of career. No doubt you are quite detailed and organized when it comes to work. Try approaching your home in the same way, paying loving attention to each nook and cranny as you clean and clear, little by little. Get a friend (or even better, a professional clutter clearer), to help if necessary.

Transiting Neptune will be entering your fourth house, or Family gua, this spring for an extended stay - where it activates your Moon in Pisces. To avoid lapsing into unconsciousness again at home, I recommend doing forgiveness work regarding early family situations or parental relations, especially your father. The March 4 New Moon will activate your Family gua; this is an ideal time to do an overhaul of this gua, bless and cleanse it, and ask for your ancestors' support in healing the past and getting things back in order.

Good luck!
Simone

Dear Simone,

During the past year, I ended a relationship with a guy I thought was my dream man, because he would not commit to a life together. Then I met a younger, foreign man. We had a fabulous time – until he moved across the country for work. I would really like to be married soon – what am I doing wrong?

Stella

Dear Stella,

You're experiencing the Neptune effect – that dreamy, elusive planet has been squaring your Jupiter (ruler of your relationship house) as well as squaring natal Neptune in your relationship house. This is a cycle of healing, creativity and spiritual growth – but it does not favor tangible commitments. In fact, it's easy to fall prey to illusions at this time, so you have to be careful while Neptune's afoot.

Rather than making yourself miserable trying to pin things down with a man, focus on your career, where Saturn is currently supporting you. It's important, however, to make Neptune your ally while he is your "houseguest." The Dec. 5 New Moon activates your Love gua, or seventh house. Set up an altar to Neptune in this gua. In addition to the pink and red items which belong here, add a blue cloth on which you place items from the sea — shells, a jar of seawater, watery images that inspire you. At the New Moon, light a blue candle to Neptune and ask for his help forgiving and releasing the past. Give thanks for his inspiration and magic. Spend time at the sea or take saltwater baths. Let Neptune dissolve your fears and desire to control outcomes, and embrace the Divine love that will heal your heart and prepare you for a commitment in 2012, when your chart favors it.

Good luck!
Simone

Contact Simone at www.astroalchemy.com to order a Quick Cast reading on your burning Astro Feng Shui question!

NEW MOONS, 2011 – 2020

(Listed in Pacific time)

2011
Jan. 4, 1:02 a.m., NM Solar Eclipse at 4 Capricorn
Feb. 2, 6:30 p.m., NM at 13 Aquarius
March 4, 12:45 p.m., NM at 13 Pisces
April 3, 7:32 a.m., NM at 13 Aries
May 3, 11:50 p.m., NM at 12 Taurus
June 1, 2:37 p.m., NM Solar Eclipse at 11 Gemini
July 1, 1:53 a.m., NM Solar Eclipse at 9 Cancer
July 30, 11:39 a.m., NM at 7 Leo
Aug. 28, 8:04 p.m., NM at 5 Virgo
Sept. 27, 4:08 a.m., NM at 4 Libra
Oct. 26, 12:55 p.m., NM at 3 Scorpio
Nov. 24, 10:09 p.m., NM at 2 Sagittarius
Dec. 24, 10:06 a.m., NM Solar Eclipse at 2 Capricorn

2012
Jan. 22, 11:39 p.m., NM at 2 Aquarius
Feb. 21, 2:34 p.m., NM at 2 Pisces
March 22, 7:37 a.m., NM at 2 Aries
April 21, 12:18 a.m., NM at 1 Taurus
May 20, 4:47 p.m., NM Solar Eclipse at 0 Gemini
June 19, 8:02 a.m., NM at 28 Gemini
July 18, 9:24 p.m., NM at 26 Cancer
Aug. 17, 8:54 a.m., NM at 25 Leo
Sept. 15, 7:10 p.m., NM at 23 Virgo
Oct. 15, 5:02 a.m., NM at 22 Libra
Nov. 13, 2:08 p.m., NM Solar Eclipse at 21 Scorpio
Dec. 13, 12:41 a.m., NM at 21 Sagittarius

2013
Jan. 11, 11:43 a.m., NM at 21 Capricorn
Feb. 9, 11:30 p.m., NM at 21 Aquarius
March 11, 12:51 p.m., NM at 21 Pisces
April 10, 2:35 a.m., NM at 20 Aries

May 9, 5:28 p.m., New Moon Solar Eclipse at 19 Taurus
June 8, 8:56 a.m., NM at 18 Gemini
July 8, 12:14 a.m., NM at 16 Cancer
Aug. 6, 2:50 p.m., NM at 14 Leo
Sept. 5, 4:36 a.m., NM at 13 Virgo
Oct. 4, 5:34 p.m., NM at 11 Libra
Nov. 3, 4:49 a.m., NM Solar Eclipse at 11 Scorpio
Dec. 2, 4:22 p.m., NM 10 Sagittarius

2014
Jan. 1, 3:14 a.m., NM 10 Capricorn
Jan. 30, 1:38 p.m., NM 10 Aquarius
Feb. 28, 11:59 p.m., NM 10 Pisces
March 30, 11:44 a.m., NM 9 Aries
April 28, 11:14 p.m., NM Solar Eclipse, 8 Taurus
May 28, 11:40 a.m., NM 7 Gemini
June 27, 1:08 a.m., NM 5 Cancer
July 26, 3:41 p.m., NM 3 Leo
Aug. 25, 7:12 a.m., NM 2 Virgo
Sept. 23, 11:13 p.m., NM 1 Libra
Oct. 23, 2:56 p.m., NM Solar Eclipse, 0 Scorpio
Nov. 22, 4:32 a.m., NM 0 Sagittarius
Dec. 21, 5:35 p.m., NM 0 Capricorn

2015
Jan. 20, 5:13 a.m., NM 0 Aquarius
Feb. 18, 3:47 p.m., NM 29 Aquarius
March 20, 2:36 a.m., NM Solar Eclipse, 29 Pisces
April 18, 11:56 a.m., NM 28 Aries
May 17, 9:13 p.m., NM 26 Taurus
June 16, 7:05 a.m., NM 25 Gemini
July 15, 6:24 p.m., NM 23 Cancer
Aug. 14, 7:53 a.m., NM 21 Leo
Sept. 12, 11:41 p.m., NM Solar Eclipse, 20 Virgo
Oct. 12, 5:05 p.m., NM 19 Libra
Nov. 11, 9:47 a.m., NM 19 Scorpio
Dec. 11, 2:29 a.m., NM 19 Sagittarius

2016

Jan. 9, 5:30 p.m., NM 19 Capricorn
Feb. 8, 6:38 a.m., NM 19 Aquarius
March 8, 5:54 p.m., NM Solar Eclipse, 18 Pisces
April 7, 4:23 a.m., NM 18 Aries
May 6, 12:29 p.m., NM 16 Taurus
June 4, 7:59 p.m., NM 14 Gemini
July 4, 4:00 a.m., NM 12 Cancer
Aug. 2, 1:44 p.m., NM 10 Leo
Sept. 1, 2:03 a.m., NM Solar Eclipse, 9 Virgo
Sept. 30, 5:11 p.m., NM 8 Libra
Oct. 30, 10:38 a.m., NM 7 Scorpio
Nov. 29, 4:18 a.m., NM 7 Sagittarius
Dec. 28, 10:53 p.m., NM 7 Capricorn

2017

Jan. 27, 4:06 p.m., NM 8 Aquarius
Feb. 26, 6:58 a.m., NM Solar Eclipse, 8 Pisces
March 27, 7:57 p.m., NM 7 Aries
April 26, 5:16 a.m., NM 6 Taurus
May 25, 12:44 p.m., NM 4 Gemini
June 23, 7:30 p.m., NM 2 Cancer
July 23, 2:45 a.m., NM 0 Leo
Aug. 21, 11:30 a.m., NM Solar Eclipse, 28 Leo
Sept. 19, 10:29 a.m., NM 27 Virgo
Oct. 19, 12:11 p.m., NM 26 Libra
Nov. 18, 3:42 a.m., NM 26 Scorpio
Dec. 17, 10:30 p.m., NM 26 Sagittarius

2018

Jan. 16, 6:17 p.m., NM 26 Capricorn
Feb. 15, 1:05 p.m., NM Solar Eclipse, 27 Aquarius
March 17, 6:11 a.m., NM 26 Pisces
April 15, 6:57 p.m., NM 26 Aries
May 15, 4:47 a.m., NM 24 Taurus
June 13, 12:43 p.m., NM 22 Gemini
July 12, 7:47 p.m., NM Solar Eclipse, 20 Cancer
Aug. 11, 2:57 a.m., NM Solar Eclipse, 18 Leo

Sept. 9, 11:01 a.m., NM 17 Virgo
Oct. 8, 8:46 p.m., NM 15 Libra
Nov. 7, 8:01 a.m., NM 15 Scorpio
Dec. 6, 11:20 p.m., NM 15 Sagittarius

2019

Jan. 5, 5:28 p.m., NM Solar Eclipse, 15 Capricorn
Feb. 4, 1:03 p.m., NM 15 Aquarius
March 6, 8:03 a.m., NM 15 Pisces
April 5, 1:50 a.m., NM 15 Aries
May 4, 3:45 p.m., NM 14 Taurus
June 3, 3:01 a.m., NM 12 Gemini
July 2, 12:16 p.m., NM Solar Eclipse, 10 Cancer
July 31, 8:11 p.m., NM 8 Leo
Aug. 30, 3:37 a.m., NM 6 Virgo
Sept. 28, 11:26 a.m., NM 5 Libra
Oct. 27, 8:38 p.m., NM 4 Scorpio
Nov. 26, 7:05 a.m., NM 4 Sagittarius
Dec. 25, 9:13 p.m., NM Solar Eclipse, 4 Capricorn

2020

Jan. 24, 1:41 p.m., NM 4 Aquarius
Feb. 23, 7:31 a.m., NM 4 Pisces
March 24, 2:28 a.m., NM 4 Aries
April 22, 7:25 p.m., NM 3 Taurus
May 22, 10:38 a.m., NM 2 Gemini
June 20, 11:41 p.m., NM Solar Eclipse, 0 Cancer
July 20, 10:32 a.m., NM 28 Cancer
Aug. 18, 7:41 p.m., NM 26 Leo
Sept. 17, 4:00 a.m., NM 25 Virgo
Oct. 16, 12:30 p.m., NM 23 Libra
Nov. 14, 9:07 p.m., NM 23 Scorpio
Dec. 14, 8:16 a.m., NM 23 Sagittarius

MERCURY RETROGRADE PERIODS, 2011 – 2020

2011: March 30-April 23, Aug. 3-Sept. 26, Nov. 24-Dec. 15
2012: March 12-April 4, July 15-Aug. 9, Nov. 6-Nov. 26
2013: Feb. 23-March 17, June 26-July 20, Oct. 21-Nov. 10
2014: Feb. 6-Feb. 28, June 7-July 2, Oct. 4-Oct. 25
2015: Jan. 21-Feb. 11, May 19-June 11, Sept. 17-Oct. 9
2016: Jan. 5-Jan. 25, April 28-May 13, Aug. 30-Sept. 22
2017: Dec. 19 2016-Jan. 8, April 9-May 3, Aug. 13-Sept. 6,
Dec. 3-Dec. 23
2018: March 23-April 15, July 26-Aug. 19, Nov. 17-Dec. 6
2019: March 5-March 28, July 7-Aug. 2, Oct. 31-Nov. 21
2020: Feb. 17-March 10, June 18-July 12, Oct. 14-Nov. 3

RECOMMENDED RESOURCES

Books:

Making the Gods Work for You by Caroline Casey
The Only Way to Learn Astrology, Vol. 1 by Marion March
Enchanted: Titania's Book of White Magic by Titania Hardie
Move Your Stuff, Change Your Life by Karen Rauch Carter
Fast Feng Shui series, by Stephanie Roberts
Space Clearing A-Z by Denise Linn
Calling in the One, by Katherine Woodward Thomas

Web sites:

www.bigskyastrology.com – April Elliot Kent's illuminating astro insights

www.Mooncircles.com – Dana Gerhardt and friends - lunar lore and features

www.Tarot.com – Many good astrology tips (including my lunar forecasts!)

www.lovingfengshui.com – Sally Adams' practical feng shui consultations

www.fastfengshui.com – Stephanie Roberts' inspirational feng shui insights

www.karenrauchcarter.com – Move Your Stuff, Change Your Life author

www.wsfs.com – Western School of Feng Shui

www.eftuniverse.com – Emotional Freedom Technique

Notes: _____

_____

_____

_____

_____

_____

_____

_____

_____

_____

_____

_____

_____

_____

_____

_____

_____

_____

_____

_____

_____

_____

_____

_____

_____

_____

_____

_____

_____

14259874R00082

Made in the USA
Lexington, KY
18 March 2012